30-SECOND
NEWTON

30-SECOND
NEWTON

The 50 key aspects of his
works, life and legacy, each
explained in half a minute

Consultant Editor
Brian Clegg

Contributors
Brian Clegg
Simon Flynn
Sophie Hebden
Andrew May

Illustrations
Ivan Hissey

Ivy Press

First published in the UK in 2016 by
Ivy Press
210 High Street, Lewes,
East Sussex BN7 2NS, UK
www.ivypress.co.uk

Copyright © The Ivy Press Limited 2016

British Library Cataloguing-in-
Publication Data
A CIP catalogue record for this
book is available from the
British Library.

ISBN: 978-1-78240-311-1

This book was conceived,
designed and produced by
Ivy Press

Creative Director **Michael Whitehead**
Publisher **Susan Kelly**
Editorial Director **Tom Kitch**
Art Director **James Lawrence**
Project Editor **Jamie Pumfrey**
Commissioning Editor **Sophie Collins**
Editor **Charles Phillips**
Designer **Ginny Zeal**
Profile & Glossary Text **Brian Clegg**

Typeset in Section

Printed and bound in China

10 9 8 7 6 5 4 3 2 1

CONTENTS

INTRODUCTION
Brian Clegg

Until Einstein came along, Isaac Newton was unrivalled as the world's most famous scientist. When the Observer newspaper put together a 'top ten' list of physicists in 2013, it was inevitable that Newton would occupy the top spot. It is ironic that Newton's word was pretty much taken as law after he became the first celebrity scientist, because part of his essential nature was a tendency to dismiss the traditional appeal to authority that had left Aristotle's distorted worldview the accepted wisdom for more than 1,500 years. Newton's independence seems to have formed at an early age. Born in Woolsthorpe Manor, a substantial farmhouse in Lincolnshire, on Christmas Day 1642 (4 January 1643 by modern dating), young Isaac had a disrupted early life. His father died before he was born, and his mother remarried when he was three, moving out to live with her new husband and leaving Newton behind with his grandparents. Later, when her second husband died, his mother returned with Newton's stepsiblings, whom he cordially disliked.

The boy's escape was education, first to school in Grantham, and then to Cambridge University, a move he made despite his mother's preference that he should stay home to look after the farm. From his early days in Cambridge there was no looking back. Newton would go on to make mathematical history by developing calculus (or the 'method of fluxions' as he called it) and in physics he was fêted for his work on light and colour, as well as the areas that made him most famous – the science of motion, forces and gravitation.

Remarkably all this seems to have been a spare-time occupation for Newton, who in the same period also worked on alchemy and theology, with a particular interest in biblical dating. This didn't prevent him having two terms as a member of parliament for Cambridge University – in 1689–90 and 1701–2, during tumultuous political times that involved the transfer of power from King James II to William of Orange. He also had a second career as Warden and then Master of the Royal Mint from 1696,

INTRODUCTION
Brian Clegg

overseeing the replacement of England's shoddy coinage and cracking down on clippers and forgers, while simultaneously taking over and reviving the country's leading scientific institution, the Royal Society.

Some scientists come to a degree of fame after their death, but Newton was enough of a celebrity to have myths emerge during his lifetime – the famous apple, for instance, certainly never fell on his head, although Newton claimed he had been inspired by seeing it fall. Newton even took part in a little rewriting of history. When he was about to be knighted, an honour granted not for services to science but for his political and fiscal work, he gave a false date for his parents' marriage to deny any possibility of his being conceived out of wedlock.

By the time Newton died in London on 20 March 1726 (31 March 1727 by current reckoning) he was so outstanding a figure that his tomb in Westminster Abbey dwarfs those of many who had enjoyed much higher status in society. This strange man with few friends and no known relationships had revealed so much of the workings of the universe that it seemed a new and beautiful mechanical creation. Even those of his theories that were dismissed at the time – such as his particle theory of light, which was pushed out by Huygens' wave theory – came back in a new form in the 20th century.

We shouldn't fall for the Victorian tendency to regard great figures of the past as thinking differently from their peers. Newton was very much of his time – but, even now, his achievements remain magnificent.

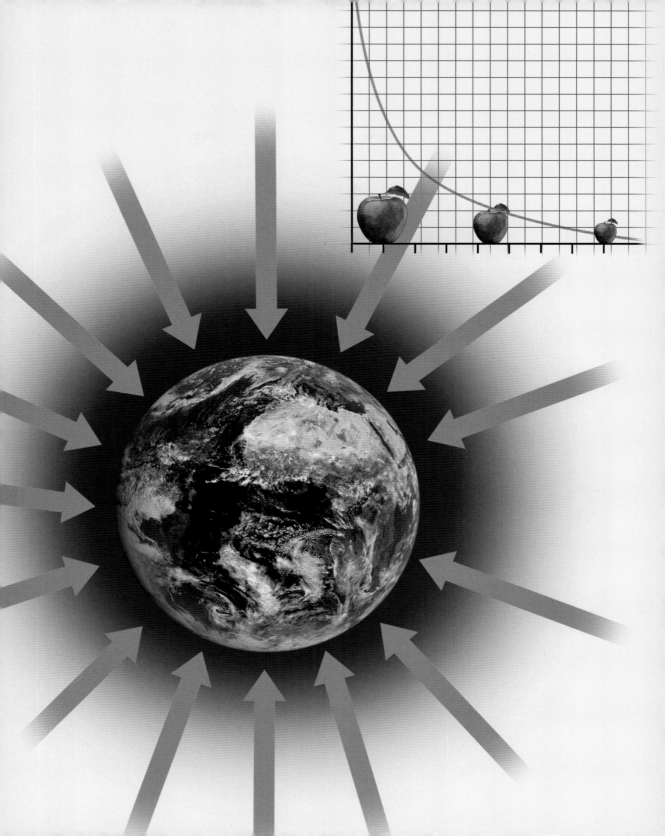

LIGHT

calculus A set of mathematical techniques developed by Newton and Leibniz, calculus has two arms. Differential calculus deals with the way one variable changes with respect to another by looking at the impact of infinitesimally small changes. Integral calculus is the inverse of differential calculus and typically might be used to work out the area under a curve. The terminology we use now is that of Leibniz – Newton called it the method of fluxions. Newton and Leibniz developed their ideas separately. Newton probably came up with fluxions first, but Leibniz published on calculus first. The result was a protracted priority dispute.

diffraction One of the properties of light used to demonstrate that it is a wave. Diffraction (which Newton called 'inflexion') occurs when light passes through a narrow aperture, or past the edge of an opaque object, resulting in waves that spread out. Newton described several diffraction experiments but struggled to explain them with his corpuscle (particle) theory of light.

ether More fully the 'luminiferous ether', or 'aether', the ether was an invisible substance that was thought to fill the universe, enabling light to cross empty space.

Hooke's *Micrographia* Newton's long-term foe, Robert Hooke, produced one of the most striking science books of the 17th century. As well as describing Hooke's ideas on light, it contained detailed drawings of his observations through an early microscope, from biological cells to the compund eye of a fly and large fold-out images of a flea and a head louse.

Gottfried Leibniz Gottfried Wilhelm Leibniz was a Leipzig-born contemporary of Newton and a consummate mathematician. His greatest achievement was the development of calculus and we still use his terminology and symbols, including the long S 'summa' or ($\int$) to represent integration in modern mathematics.

Newton's letter on light and colour A letter written by Newton in February 1672 to Henry Oldenburg, secretary of the Royal Society, and published in *Philosophical Transactions*, describing Newton's findings when experimenting with light.

Newton's theory of colour and light
Newton revolutionized our understanding of light and colour. He was the first to realize that white light is a mix of the colours of the spectrum, that different colours bend to different degrees when passing from one substance to another – and so produce a rainbow when passing through a prism or raindrop – and that the colour of an object represents the remaining light when the object has absorbed other colours from white light.

Opticks The second of Newton's great books, *Opticks* was published in English in 1704. The full title is *Opticks, or a treatise of the reflexions, refractions, inflexions and colours of light. Also two treatises of the species and magnitude of curvilinear figures.*

Principia Newton's masterpiece, *Philosophiæ Naturalis Principia Mathematica* ('Mathematical Principles of Natural Philosophy'), gave us his three laws of motion and his law of universal gravitation, showing that the same principle is responsible for an apple falling and for planets orbiting the Sun. The book was published in 1687 in Latin.

reflector A reflecting telescope, like Newton's, using a curved mirror to collect light instead of a lens. Newton's telescope focused the light on a small flat mirror that reflected the image out of the side of the telescope, whereas the earlier reflector proposed by Scottish astronomer James Gregory used a small curved mirror to reflect the image out through a hole in the middle of the main mirror.

wave theory of light/Newton's particle theory Newton's contemporaries, notably Dutch scientist Christiaan Huygens, thought that light was a wave. Newton never accepted this and although he kept his observations on light and colour separate from his hypotheses on the nature of light, he made detailed arguments for light to be made up of particles. Ironically, he was proved wrong in the 19th century, only to have a particle model become more accepted with quantum theory in the 20th century.

THE REFLECTING TELESCOPE

the 30-second theory

RELATED TOPICS
See also
THE ROYAL SOCIETY
page 18

THE STOURBRIDGE PRISM
page 36

From his optical experiments, Newton knew that when white light passes through a lens its component colours are bent, or refracted, by different amounts – a phenomenon known as chromatic aberration. The effect is not large, but it meant that the refracting telescopes of the day, made with lenses, were unable to produce a perfectly clear image. In 1663 a Scotsman named James Gregory had proposed an alternative type of telescope, using curved mirrors instead of lenses, and Newton realized that Gregory's reflecting telescope would be free from chromatic aberration. There were practical difficulties, however, which had prevented Gregory from actually building his telescope. Newton simplified the design, replacing one of the curved mirrors with a flat one, and produced a small prototype in 1668. It proved to be just as powerful as a much larger refracting telescope. One of Newton's Cambridge colleagues, Isaac Barrow, suggested the new instrument should be brought to the attention of the Royal Society in London. This prompted Newton to build a second, larger telescope – still only 23 cm (9 in) long and 5 cm (2 in) diameter – which Barrow demonstrated in London in 1671. The telescope so impressed the members of the Society that they elected Newton to a fellowship a few months later.

3-SECOND THRASH
Newton invented a new kind of telescope, using a curved mirror instead of a lens to focus incoming light.

3-MINUTE THOUGHT
Newton was mistaken in his belief that a lens free from chromatic aberration could never be constructed. The problem was eventually solved by John Dollond, using a compound lens made from different types of glass. Nevertheless, most astronomical telescopes – including the Hubble Space Telescope – are reflectors, working on a similar principle to Newton's original design, because it is much easier to fabricate a large mirror than a lens of the same size.

3-SECOND BIOGRAPHIES
ISAAC BARROW
1630–77
English mathematician who showed Newton's telescope to the Royal Society

JAMES GREGORY
1638–75
Scottish astronomer who designed but never built a reflecting telescope

JOHN DOLLOND
1706–61
English optician who, after Newton's death, solved the problem of chromatic aberration

30-SECOND TEXT
Andrew May

One small, flat mirror and one slightly larger, curved one produced the effect for which Newton was looking.

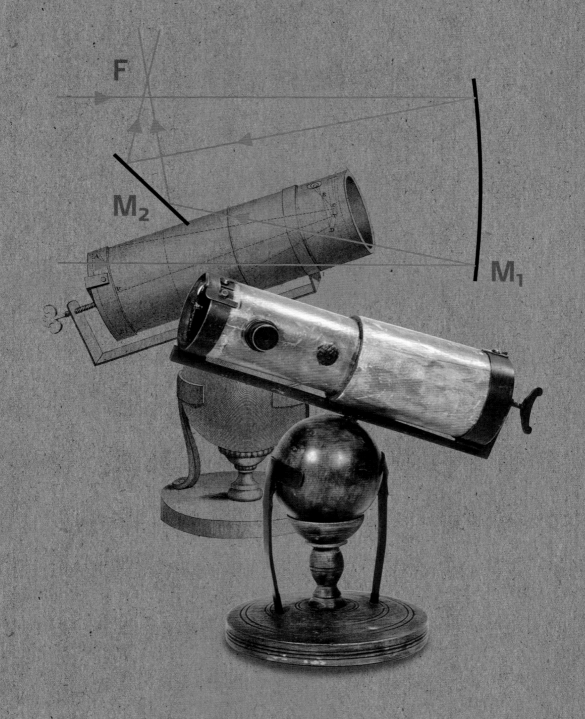

F

M₂

M₁

EXPERIMENTS ON THE EYE

the 30-second theory

3-SECOND THRASH
Newton performed some painful, brutal and potentially damaging experiments on his own eyes, including one in which he inserted an object between his eye and its socket.

3-MINUTE THOUGHT
Science has a remarkable history of people experimenting on themselves. Humphry Davy investigated the effects of laughing gas (nitrous oxide) on himself – a poem he wrote afterwards suggests he rather enjoyed the experience; Pierre Curie taped radium salts to his arm for ten hours; Werner Forssmann inserted a catheter in a vein, pushed it all the way to his heart and then took an X-ray of it.

When it came to performing scientific experiments, Newton was very much prepared to put his body on the line. This included staring at the Sun reflected in a mirror with one eye until all pale objects seemed to take on the colour red and dark ones blue. Even when this sensation ceased, he was able to recover this 'fantasie' by closing his eye and imagining he was looking at the Sun. It took Newton four days to recover his sight to an acceptable level, and he had recurring problems over the following months. Even more astonishingly, Newton also physically interfered with his own sight. In notes written in 1665–66, Newton describes an experiment in which he inserted a bodkin (a little like a knitting needle) between his eye and its socket as near to the back of the eye as possible. He then pressed so as to change the retina's curvature, resulting in his seeing 'white darke & coloured circles' as he continued to vary the pressure and movement. Newton was not alone among his contemporaries in viewing his own body as a legitimate entity on which to experiment, but his dedication to the cause is unquestionable given the pain he must have subsequently suffered.

RELATED TOPICS
See also
RECOMBINATION
page 42

THE NATURE OF COLOUR
page 48

3-SECOND BIOGRAPHIES
HUMPHRY DAVY
1778–1829
British chemist and inventor, President of the Royal Society 1820–27

PIERRE CURIE
1859–1906
French physicist, winner of the Nobel Prize in Physics in 1903 along with his wife, Marie, and Henri Becquerel

WERNER FORSSMANN
1904–79
German physician, member of the Nazi Party 1932–45 and winner of the Nobel Prize in Medicine in 1956

30-SECOND TEXT
Simon Flynn

Newton's sun-gazing made pale objects appear red and darker ones blue. His eyes needed several days to recover.

THE ROYAL SOCIETY

the 30-second theory

Newton was first elected to the Royal Society in 1672, the year in which his letter on light and colour was published. In 1703, he became the Royal Society's 12th president, following in the footsteps of men such as Christopher Wren and Samuel Pepys, and would remain in the position until his death. Just over 40 years old when Newton took over, the Society was very much in need of a shot in the arm and Newton was just the man to provide it. He revived the fortunes of the Society, which was virtually bankrupt, and oversaw the purchase of its first home. His second great work, the *Opticks*, was published in 1704 and was dedicated to the Royal Society. Newton would go on to shape the future of the Society and establish his own reputation once and for all. Heaven help those who got in his way. When the priority dispute regarding the invention of calculus boiled over in 1708 with Leibniz, who was also a fellow of the Society, Newton set up a committee to clear up the matter once and for all. It wasn't a fair fight – Newton wrote the committee's report. In 1709, Newton drew up a 'hit list' of fellows he wished to remove from the Society's council. Needless to say, none of them were re-elected later that year.

3-SECOND THRASH
Newton was President of the Royal Society for the last 24 years of his life. He served it well – and it served him even better.

3-MINUTE THOUGHT
The roots of the Royal Society lie in the work of Sir Francis Bacon, considered by many to be 'the father of experimental science'. Bacon had wanted to create an administration of learning and described an institution 'dedicated to the study of the works and creatures of God'. The inaugural meeting of the Royal Society took place in 1660, less than 40 years after Bacon's death. The Society's motto is *nullius in verba* (roughly translated as 'take nobody's word for it').

RELATED TOPICS
See also
THE REFLECTING TELESCOPE
page 14

ROYAL MINT
page 56

GOTTFRIED LEIBNIZ
page 66

3-SECOND BIOGRAPHIES
FRANCIS BACON
1561–1626
Philosopher and Lord Chancellor of England

CHRISTOPHER WREN
1632–1723
Architect of St Paul's Cathedral and founding member of the Royal Society

SAMUEL PEPYS
1633–1703
Diarist, MP and President of the Royal Society 1684–86

30-SECOND TEXT
Simon Flynn

Nullius in verba – *the Royal Society's Latin motto – celebrates fellows' determination to verify statements by experiment.*

STANDING ON THE SHOULDERS OF GIANTS

the 30-second theory

Within a week of Newton's theory of colour and light being made public in 1672, Robert Hooke, the Royal Society's first Curator of Experiments, presented a detailed critique of it based on his own experiments with prisms along with work previously published in his *Micrographia*. One significant difference between the two was that Hooke argued for a wave theory of light, whereas Newton appeared to favour a particle theory. Hooke was also convinced that colour was the result of light being modified. Three years later, Newton wrote an 'Hypothesis of Light', mentioning Hooke in his covering letter. When it was read out at the Royal Society, Hooke stood up and declared that most of what had been said could be found in his *Micrographia*, which Newton 'had only carried farther in some particulars'. Newton was incensed. In an effort to prevent things from boiling over in public, Hooke suggested that he and Newton correspond privately regarding their respective views on optics. Newton concurred and replied that 'if I have seen further it is by standing on the shoulders of giants'. The peace, however, wasn't to last and tempers flared again in the run-up to the publication of Newton's magnum opus, the *Principia*, 11 years later. It was only after Hooke died in 1703 that Newton chose to publish his second great work, *Opticks*.

RELATED TOPICS
See also
THE ETHER
page 22

ROBERT HOOKE
page 24

PARTICLES OF LIGHT
page 26

EXPERIMENTUM CRUCIS
page 40

3-SECOND BIOGRAPHIES
ROBERT HOOKE
1635–1703
English natural philosopher and architect

EDMUND HALLEY
1656–1742
English astronomer and the second Astronomer Royal, who funded the publication of Newton's *Principia*

30-SECOND TEXT
Simon Flynn

Hooke, a great polymath, was surveyor to the City of London as well as a natural philosopher; he published **Micrographia** *in 1665.*

3-SECOND THRASH
Newton's first published work kick-started an intellectual feud with Robert Hooke that would continue to peak and trough until the latter's death 30 years later.

3-MINUTE THOUGHT
Hooke's comments regarding the *Principia* hurt Newton deeply. The astronomer Edmund Halley informed him that Hooke was making claims that Newton had got the idea of gravity's strength being proportional to the inverse square of the distance between two objects from him and therefore wanted acknowledgment of his priority. In response, Newton removed or reduced many acknowledgments of Hooke he *had* included – such as from *Clarissimus Hookius* ('the most distinguished Hooke') to just *Hookius*.

MICROGRAPHIA

OR SOME

Physiological Descriptions

OF

MINUTE BODIES

MADE BY

MAGNIFYING GLASSES.

OBSERVATIONS and INQUIRIES thereupon.

By R. HOOKE, Fellow of the Royal Society.

THE ETHER

the 30-second theory

The ancient idea of a medium called the ether that permeates all of space and matter was used by Descartes in 1644 – when Newton was a toddler aged two – to explain the circular motion of the planets and as a propagation medium for light. Descartes thought of the ether as a vortex of particles on which the planets float like leaves in a whirlpool of water. He considered light to be a travelling pressure in the ether, with colours produced when ether particles rotate. Newton's contemporaries used the ether to explain interactions between bodies without any direct contact – like magnetism and gravity. Newton's nemesis, Robert Hooke, described light as a vibration or pulse of the ether. The Dutch scientist Christiaan Huygens took Hooke's ideas further, describing light as a wave propagating through the ether. Newton disagreed with the wave hypothesis for the simple reason that light does not turn corners. He imagined light as globules, or 'corpuscles' of various sizes that are emitted from shining bodies and travel at a finite speed until they enter the eye. He suggested that the ether consists of particles smaller than particles of air or light that are 'more strongly elastic'.

RELATED TOPICS
See also
PARTICLES OF LIGHT
page 26

THE STOURBRIDGE PRISM
page 36

PLANETARY MOTION
page 136

3-SECOND BIOGRAPHIES
RENÉ DESCARTES
1596–1650
French philosopher, mathematician and scientist.

CHRISTIAAN HUYGENS
1629–95
Dutch mathematician, developer of the wave theory of light.

30-SECOND TEXT
Sophie Hebden

3-SECOND THRASH
Newton imagined light to consist of globules that are emitted by shining bodies and then travel through the ether in straight lines until they enter the eye.

3-MINUTE THOUGHT
Newton didn't like talking about the ether or what light consists of – he admitted he didn't know what the ether really was, and used it in the absence of a better explanation. Later in life he dispensed with the ether altogether as a propagating medium for light and rejected Descartes' celestial vortex – Newton's theories of motion would explain planetary motion perfectly well without it.

Light 'corpuscles' travel from source to eye through ether, with colours produced when particles in the ether rotate.

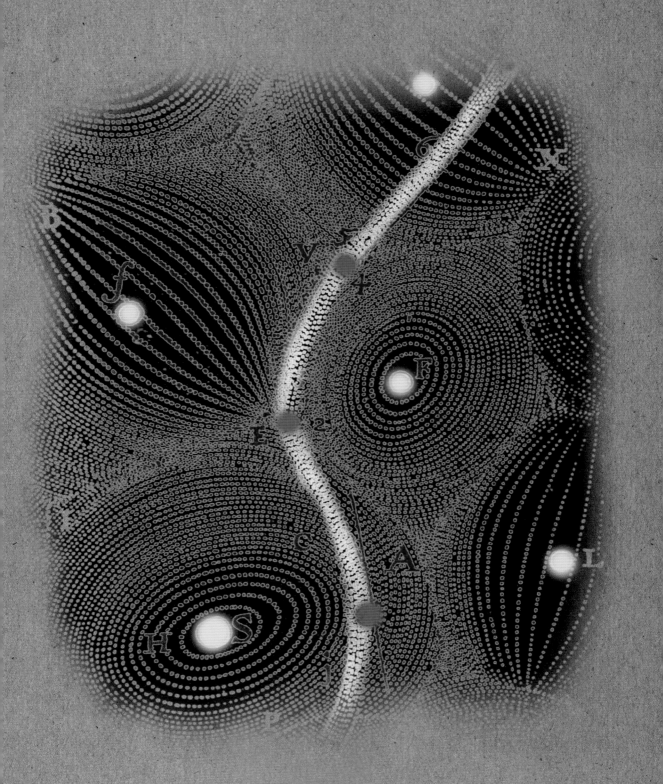

18 July 1635
Born in Freshwater on the Isle of Wight

1648
Sent to London as apprentice to Peter Lely, but soon joins Westminster School

1653
Goes up to Christ Church College, Oxford

5 November 1662
Becomes Curator of Experiments at the Royal Society

3 June 1663
Becomes fellow of the Royal Society

1664/5
Becomes professor of geometry at Gresham College, London

1665
Micrographia published

1666
Assists Wren in rebuilding London after the Great Fire

1672
First encounter with Newton over light and colour

1678
Publishes *Of Springs*, giving his law of elasticity

1679
First writes to Newton about his ideas on gravitation

1690
Accuses Newton of plagiarism during a lecture at the Royal Society

3 March 1703
Dies in London

ROBERT HOOKE

Robert Hooke was Newton's best-known adversary, with battles lasting from Newton's first submission to the Royal Society to Hooke's death.

Young Hooke was expected to follow his father and uncles into the clergy, but he suffered persistent headaches, ending his education and leaving him to explore nature and the mechanical devices that fascinated him. When at the age of 13 he lost his father, it was decided that, as a capable draughtsman, the boy should be apprenticed to Peter Lely, a London portrait painter. This did not last long. Showing the self-determination evident throughout his life, Hooke used his £40 legacy to pay for a place at Westminster School.

Moving on to Christ Church College, Oxford, Hooke explored astronomy and mechanics, but most importantly worked for proto-chemist Robert Boyle, a member of the 'invisible college' whose members included John Wallis and Christopher Wren. When political changes made it difficult for the 'college' members to remain in Oxford, many moved to Gresham College, London, where they helped formed the Royal Society. In 1662 Hooke was appointed Curator of Experiments.

Then in 1665 Hooke combined his draughtsmanship with scientific explorations, publishing *Micrographia*, a wonderfully illustrated book featuring large fold-out drawings rendering the likes of a flea with horrible accuracy. In the same book he noted the repeating structure of tree bark, calling the box shapes 'cells' as they reminded him of monks' cells. Hooke would achieve much in his own right, from constructing the first practical Gregorian telescope to delineating his law of elasticity. But for us his main role was as adversary to Newton.

When Newton's letter on light and colour was presented to the Royal Society, Hooke was asked to check it out. He later admitted spending little time on it, claiming the parts he thought right were based on his own ideas, while the rest was wrong. Hooke had repeated encounters with Newton until his death, mostly acrimonious, leading Newton to write his famous 'standing on the shoulders of giants' line, thought to be an insult to Hooke's physique. This enmity was still clear in 1690, when Hooke gave a lecture in which he commented on the theory of gravitation, which 'I myself first discovered and showed to this Society … which of late Mr Newton has done the favour to print and publish as his own inventions.' Hooke was once underestimated, but his true place in the history of science is now recognized.

Brian Clegg

PARTICLES OF LIGHT

the 30-second theory

On the periphery of Newton's optics work were his ideas about the intrinsic nature of light. He imagined that light is emitted from shining bodies as streams of tiny particles called 'corpuscles'. These travel away from shining bodies at high speed in a straight line, and when they enter the eye they produce an image of an object. The corpuscular theory succeeded at explaining the reflection of light off surfaces, but struggled when it came to other phenomena, such as the bending or refraction of light in glass, and diffraction – how light is bent at a sharp edge. In his major book about light called *Opticks*, published in 1704, Newton tried to explain these phenomena by employing the ether. He suggested that the ether transmits vibrations faster than the speed of light, and so when light corpuscles are overtaken by the vibrations of the ether at a surface they are put into 'fits of easy reflection' and 'fits of easy transmission', which cause refraction and diffraction. These ideas were highly speculative, and an alternative wave theory developed by Christiaan Huygens gave a better explanation for these phenomena. Partly due to Newton's scientific prestige, the corpuscular view dominated for the next 100 years.

Optical insights – Newton used his conception of the ether to make the corpuscular theory of light fit with diffraction and refraction effects.

OPTICKS:
OR, A
TREATISE
OF THE
REFLEXIONS, REFRACTIONS,
INFLEXIONS and COLOURS
OF
LIGHT.
ALSO
Two TREATISES
OF THE
SPECIES and MAGNITUDE
OF
Curvilinear Figures.

INVENTING DATA

the 30-second theory

Although not the first to base his theories on observation and experiment – Galileo, for instance, made big steps in this direction – Newton was an early exponent of this centrepiece of modern scientific practice. This was not entirely new. Astronomers, particularly, had made many measurements and recorded much data, but the ancient Greek tendency to base theory on argument rather than evidence still largely held sway. Newton was harsh in his assessment of the Greco-Roman astronomer Ptolemy. There was a suspicion that Ptolemy had passed off someone else's data (probably Hipparchus, whose writings were lost) as his own. Newton accused Ptolemy of inventing data to fit his theories, writing that he perpetrated 'a crime committed against fellow scientists and scholars, a betrayal of the ethics and integrity of his profession that has forever deprived mankind of fundamental information about an important area of astronomy and history'. Newton added 'Instead of abandoning the theories, he deliberately fabricated observations from the theories so that he could claim that the observations prove the validity of his theories. In every scientific or scholarly setting known, this practice is called fraud, and it is a crime against science and scholarship.'

RELATED TOPICS
See also
THE STOURBRIDGE PRISM
page 36

THE SECOND PRISM
page 38

EXPERIMENTUM CRUCIS
page 40

3-SECOND BIOGRAPHIES
CLAUDIUS PTOLEMY
c.85–c.165
Egyptian-born Greco-Roman astronomer

FRANCIS LINE
1595–1675
English Jesuit mathematician working in Liège

EDME MARIOTTE
1620–84
French natural philosopher

30-SECOND TEXT
Brian Clegg

3-SECOND THRASH
Newton was dismissive of those who invented data to support their theories, reflecting the increasing importance of observation and experiment to the scientific method.

3-MINUTE THOUGHT
When others tried to replicate Newton's experiments on light in which the coloured light from a first prism is passed through a second, they did not reproduce his results. Newton admitted both that his description of the experiment was not sufficiently detailed and that he sometimes saw colours change when passing through a second prism, but chose to ignore this. He accepted the data that supported his theory and ignored the rest, which would now be called 'cherry picking'.

Despite his forthright condemnation of Ptolemy, Newton was himself guilty of picking and choosing data in his light experiments.

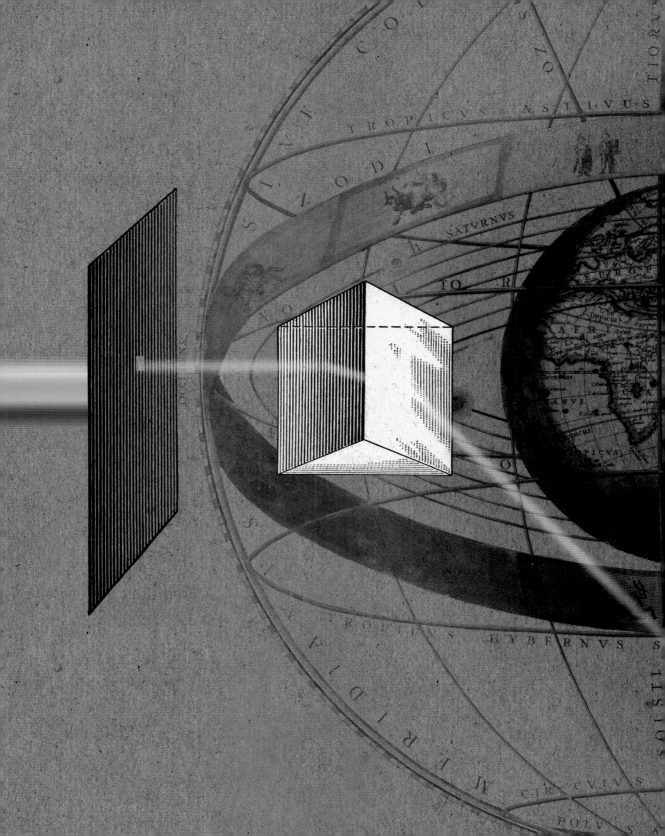

COLOUR

chromatic aberration Because different colours of light bend to different degrees when moving between, say, air and glass, a simple lens produces coloured fringes rather than a clear image: this is called chromatic aberration.

concave A curved surface that bends inwards, typically in a concave lens.

convex A curved surface that bends outwards, typically in a convex lens.

René Descartes French philosopher and natural philosopher who thought that light was transmitted by a series of tiny rigid spheres in the ether, so that a 'push' from a source of light would produce an instantaneous push on the viewer's eye causing sight, and that gravity was caused by spinning vortices in the ether. More valuably, Descartes showed how to link geometric forms and algebraic equations, enabling a more powerful numerical approach to understanding nature, rather than the traditional use of geometry.

diatonic scale A musical scale that takes seven steps to go from a note to the same note an octave higher, typified by the white keys on a piano. The C major diatonic scale goes CDEFGAB before returning to C. Newton felt that light ought to have an equivalent seven colours.

Opus Majus A medieval masterpiece of science, written by the English friar Roger Bacon in 1267. Originally intended to be a proposal for an encyclopedia of science to send to the pope in the hope of obtaining funds, the *Opus Majus* grew into a 500,000-word tour de force that gives one of the best pictures of scientific knowledge in medieval Europe, along with Bacon's original ideas.

Ignace-Gaston Pardies Ignace-Gaston Pardies was a French contemporary of Newton's. Unlike Descartes, he believed that the speed of light was finite and that light was a kind of harmonic vibration that produced wavelike effects. Pardies initially disputed Newton's explanation of how white light was made up of the spectrum of colours, but Newton won him round. Newton's arch-enemy, Robert Hooke, used this dispute in his attack on Newton.

prism Geometrically, a prism is a three-dimensional shape made by extending a polygon into a third dimension, so it has two flat 'ends'. Optically it is a transparent object, typically glass, with surfaces at an angle to each other, so light can be refracted as it passes in through one face and again as it passes out through another. The most common form is the triangular prism, a triangle extended in the third dimension to make a block.

refraction The change of direction of a beam of light as it passes from one substance into another, for example between air and glass, or air and water. Refraction is caused by a change in speed of the light in the different media, and results in bending in towards a perpendicular line from the surface when the light goes into a substance in which it travels more slowly.

spectra A rainbow is a spectrum (plural spectra) – it refers to a range within a continuous set of values. This can in principle be anything (for example, the political spectrum), but in light refers to a range of colours of light, corresponding to differing wavelengths, frequencies or energies of photons (all three are equivalent). The full spectrum of light goes from radio, through microwaves, infrared, visible, ultraviolet and X-rays all the way up to gamma rays. Visible light is only a tiny part of the whole spectrum.

spherical aberration Early lenses often had shapes that were like a section of a sphere, but this is not ideal because rays of light near the edges of the lens don't focus at exactly the same point as rays near the centre: this is called spherical aberration.

uncompounded light/compounded light
Newton distinguished between 'uncompounded light', which had a single colour, and 'compounded light' like white light, which was a mix of colours. We would now say that uncompounded light has a single frequency, wavelength or energy of photons.

COLOURS OF THE RAINBOW

the 30-second theory

Whenever we see a rainbow, we instantly think of it comprising seven colours: red, orange, yellow, green, blue, indigo and violet. This is all thanks to Newton and his experiments using prisms. His first lectures as Lucasian Professor of Mathematics at Cambridge were on optics (*Lectiones opticae*), which included his earliest experiments using a prism. He initially only described five colours, but when he came to revise them he chose to include orange and indigo in an effort to provide 'a more refined symmetry' and show a connection between colour and music. He argued that colours could form harmonies in much the same way the seven notes of the diatonic scale did. In a letter published by the Royal Society at the same time, Newton acknowledged an 'indefinite variety of intermediate shades' but curiously chose not to highlight the arbitrary nature of his division when he came to write his *Opticks* more than 30 years later. Quite what colours Newton might have listed if he'd been living a couple of centuries earlier is unclear as orange didn't exist as a specific colour until the 15th century when it took its name from the fruit. Up until that point, it would have been referred to as yellow-red.

RELATED TOPICS
See also
THE ROYAL SOCIETY
page 18

THE STOURBRIDGE PRISM
page 36

3-SECOND BIOGRAPHY
WILLIAM HERSCHEL
1738–1822
German-born British musician and astronomer who discovered infrared while investigating the reaction of a thermometer at different positions on a spectrum

30-SECOND TEXT
Simon Flynn

3-SECOND THRASH
Newton initially thought there to be five colours, then seven with 'innumerable intermediate gradations' before seeming to stress *only* seven.

3-MINUTE THOUGHT
Today, we know that the colours we see form just a tiny fraction of the electromagnetic spectrum, which also includes radio waves, microwaves, infrared, ultraviolet, X-rays and gamma rays. In 1800, the astronomer William Herschel discovered infrared by accident when conducting experiments with a prism. It is estimated that the human eye can differentiate approximately 10 million colours. Newton was well aware there were more than seven.

The seven colours familiar from the rainbow were identified by Newton through his prism experiments.

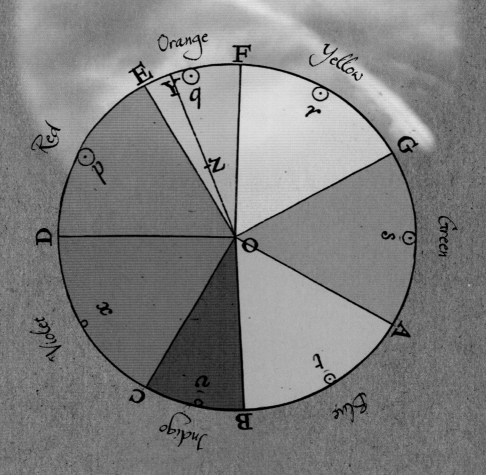

THE STOURBRIDGE PRISM

the 30-second theory

In the early 1660s, the dominant explanation of light and colour was that of French natural philosopher René Descartes. It was assumed by almost everyone that light in its simplest and most natural form was white and that colour resulted from a modification of white light – an apple would appear red because its surface changed the physical properties of the white light hitting it. In a series of brilliant experiments involving a prism Newton said he bought at the Stourbridge Fair just outside Cambridge in 1665, Newton turned the accepted theory of colours completely on its head. He described an experiment in which a hole was made in his window shutter such that his room was dark except for a ray of light from this hole; the prism was placed so that the light passed through it, resulting in a rainbow being cast on the opposite wall. Crucially, the spectrum formed appeared oblong in shape and stopped at its sides. According to Descartes' theory, a circle would have instead been formed. This convinced Newton that Descartes was wrong. Now he had to develop his own theory of light and colour.

3-SECOND THRASH
Before Newton, people believed colour was the result of the properties of white light being modified.

3-MINUTE THOUGHT
Newton tells us that he originally bought the prism to help with his work on the grinding of non-spherical lenses. Descartes had demonstrated that spherical lenses are unable to focus images perfectly. This had significant implications for telescopes and microscopes. Newton's work on his reflecting telescope had taken significant strides in reducing the spherical lens aberrations. It's possible to approximate a concave lens by placing two prisms point-to-point and a convex lens by having two prisms base-to-base.

RELATED TOPICS
See also
PARTICLES OF LIGHT
page 26

COLOURS OF THE RAINBOW
page 34

THE SECOND PRISM
page 38

EXPERIMENTUM CRUCIS
page 40

THE NATURE OF COLOUR
page 48

3-SECOND BIOGRAPHY
RENÉ DESCARTES
1596–1650
French natural philosopher whose mechanistic view of science dominated the mid-17th century.

30-SECOND TEXT
Simon Flynn

Newton's experiment with the Stourbridge prism produced an rectangular spectrum rather than a circular array of colours.

THE SECOND PRISM

the 30-second theory

Having convinced himself that Descartes' theory of light and colour was wrong, Newton now had to formulate his own theory. He felt it vital to rule out the possibility that his results had been due to imperfections in the prism and exhibited his experimental genius by adding a second prism to his investigations: if irregularities were the cause of his previous observations, it would be impossible for a second refraction, involving a second prism, to *undo* these. Repeating the 'Stourbridge prism' experiment, he took a second, similarly sized prism and inverted it with respect to the first in such a way that when the light left the second prism it was as if it hadn't been refracted at all – the second prism remixed the spectrum from the first back into white light. He then set the two prisms up so that the spectral light entering the second prism was refracted even more: red light that entered the second prism remained red, and blue light remained blue, when they left. In this series of brilliant experiments, Newton's introduction of a second prism made all the difference in exploring the nature of light.

RELATED TOPICS
See also
PARTICLES OF LIGHT
page 26

COLOURS OF THE RAINBOW
page 34

THE STOURBRIDGE PRISM
page 36

EXPERIMENTUM CRUCIS
page 40

THE NATURE OF COLOUR
page 48

3-SECOND BIOGRAPHY
RENÉ DESCARTES
1596–1650
French natural philosopher

30-SECOND TEXT
Simon Flynn

3-SECOND THRASH
In a series of compelling experiments involving more that one prism, Newton showed white light to be made up of a mixture of colours.

3-MINUTE THOUGHT
One problem with reproducing prism-based experiments during the 17th century was the variable quality of the glassworks. They were typically small and often riddled with imperfections such as bubbles – and the sides were rarely perfectly flat. If you think school experiments based on Newton are often unsatisfactory, imagine the problems faced by contemporary readers of his work. This is one of the reasons why Newton's ideas weren't immediately embraced by other natural philosophers.

Newton's second prism was set up so that the spectral light entering it was refracted even more, confirming light to be made of a mixture of colours.

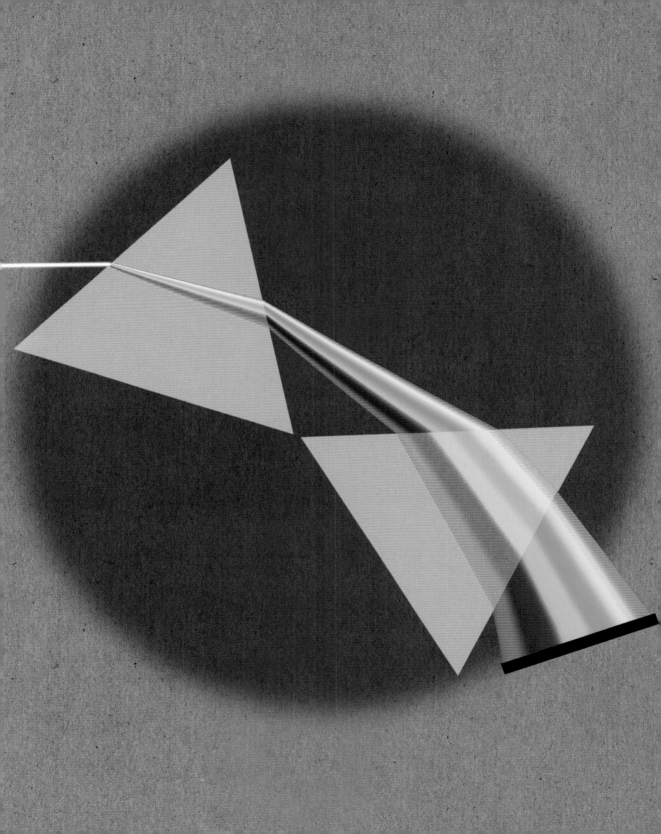

EXPERIMENTUM CRUCIS

the 30-second theory

In February 1672 Newton wrote a long letter to the Royal Society in London narrating the experiments with light he had conducted at home in Woolsthorpe and in Cambridge. He included diagrams showing how a ray of sunlight from a hole in the window shutter bent as it passed through a prism, producing an elongated colour spectrum on the wall, blue at the far end, red nearest to a straight path. He then described – and showed in the drawing – how he put a second prism in the path of a coloured beam, to see if blue or red light could be split into further colours. The coloured rays bent on passing through the second prism but did not create new colours: blue stayed blue, red stayed red. This, Newton stated in Latin rather pompously, was his *experimentum crucis* ('critical experiment'): it showed that the colours are 'pure' and that white sunlight comprises a mixture of these colours; the glass doesn't modify the light or create the colours, it simply separates them. The differences in the degree of bending that each colour undergoes helps to sort them out: blue is bent or 'refracted' through a greater angle than red.

RELATED TOPICS
See also
THE STOURBRIDGE PRISM
page 36

THE RAINBOW
page 46

THE NATURE OF COLOUR
page 48

3-SECOND BIOGRAPHIES
FRANCIS BACON
1561–1626
English philosopher who coined the phrase *experimentum crucis*

ROBERT HOOKE
1635–1703
English natural philosopher and architect, who adapted the phrase from Bacon; Newton probably borrowed it from Hooke

30-SECOND TEXT
Sophie Hebden

3-SECOND THRASH
Newton summed up his experiment thus: 'Light consists of rays differently refrangible.'

3-MINUTE THOUGHT
Using a piece of glass to produce the colours of the rainbow wasn't a new idea – people noticed that this could be done as soon as glass was invented. But taking it a step further with a second prism enabled Newton to see beyond the prevailing wisdom – and try new things, like combining different colours to see what happened.

The critical experiment – while the first prism separates white light into the spectrum of colours, the second does not split them further.

RECOMBINATION

the 30-second theory

It might seem that Newton's use of a pair of prisms to investigate a beam of sunlight was conclusive. When he put any individual colour from the spectrum produced by one prism through a second, and found the colour was unchanged, you might imagine that he had the topic sewn up. But because the idea that the colours of the spectrum were all in white light ran so contrary to the accepted notions of the day, Newton had to reinforce his findings. To do this, he devised a recombination experiment. Realizing that a lens would focus the spread of colours onto the point, he put a lens into the path of a prism-produced spectrum and showed that the resultant, recombined colours produced a white outcome. (This was, according to Newton, 'a Lens of about three foot radius'.) To hammer the effect home, he used a fine comb to remove different parts of the spectrum before the light hit the lens, showing that the colour of the resultant blob of light varied with the components of the spectrum that went to make it up. It took the whole array to produce apparently simple white light.

RELATED TOPICS
See also
THE STOURBRIDGE PRISM
page 36

THE SECOND PRISM
page 38

THE NATURE OF COLOUR
page 48

3-SECOND BIOGRAPHIES
ARISTOTLE
384–322BC
Ancient Greek philosopher whose ideas on science (including light) were largely accepted until Galileo and Newton's time

IGNACE-GASTON PARDIES
1636–73
Parisian Jesuit and philosopher who initially dismissed Newton's idea that white light was made up of a combination of the colours of the spectrum

30-SECOND TEXT
Brian Clegg

3-SECOND THRASH
By sending a full spectrum of light through a lens, Newton was able to underline the way the set of colours combined to produce white light.

3-MINUTE THOUGHT
The idea that white light was made up of a combination of the colours of the spectrum was particularly uncomfortable for contemporaries of Newton like the French philosopher Pardies, as classical Greek physics still held sway in the universities. According to Aristotle, whose physics was pretty much accepted unchanged for 1,500 years, all the colours were the result of different surfaces reacting to a mix of light and darkness, making white light a fundamental, rather than a composite.

With a substantial lens ('about three foot radius'), Newton recombined the colours of the spectrum.

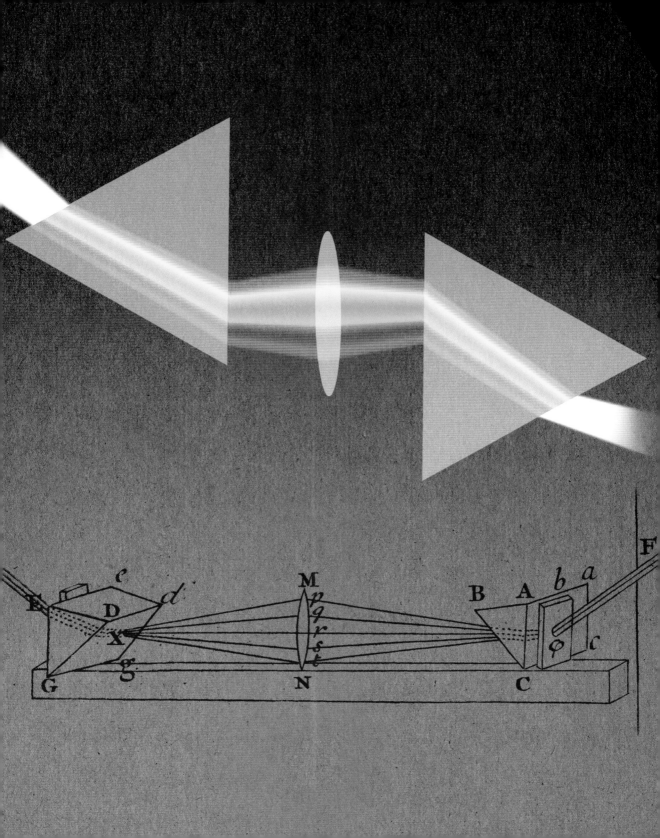

14 April 1629
Born in The Hague

1645
Attends the University
of Leiden

1647
Moves to the College of
Orange in Breda

1654
Returns to Hofwijck, the
family home in The Hague

1655
Discovers Titan, a moon
of Saturn

1656
Constructs a prototype
pendulum clock

1657
Writes a treatise on
probability

1663
Elected a fellow of the
Royal Society

1666
Moves to Paris and the
French Academy of
Sciences

1678
First discusses his wave
theory of light

1681
Returns to The Hague

1684
Designs the skeletal
'aerial' telescope

1689
Visits England and meets
Newton

1690
Publishes his great work
on light, *Traité de la
Lumière* ('Treatise on
Light')

8 July 1695
Dies in The Hague

CHRISTIAAN HUYGENS

Of all his adversaries, Newton seems to have had most respect for Christiaan Huygens. This Dutch scientist studied everything from probability theory to astronomy, where he discovered Saturn's moon Titan, but Newton was primarily interested in his expertise on light.

Huygens' father was a wealthy diplomat who moved in circles that admitted Galileo and Descartes. Like many privileged children of the period, Huygens had private tutors to prepare him for university. At the University of Leiden he studied law and mathematics, with the intention of following his father into a diplomatic career. He did, in fact, start down this path – but maths proved his passion at university and Huygens was able to make use of his private income to devote himself to study and experiment.

Huygens' early work was primarily in mathematics, but over time he developed an interest in astronomy, grinding his own lenses and devising a new form of eyepiece, though for his observations he often made use of professionally constructed telescopes. His interests broadened, leading to his development of the pendulum clock. From 1666 to 1681 he lived in Paris, involved with the then new French Academy of Sciences, founded by Louis XIV.

As a fellow of the Royal Society, Huygens saw Newton's early work on light and colour. He was very supportive of Newton's explanation of colour, but criticized the hypothesis that light was composed of particles. Huygens was sure that light was a wave, which meant it needed a material to 'wave' in. He believed that apparently empty space was filled, in effect, with vast quantities of tiny elastic spheres, making up the ether. When a source generated light it started off as a movement in a single sphere, which influenced other spheres around it. The result was a picture of light moving outwards as a collection of tiny wavelets, each triggering new wavelets from the spheres around it. Many of these would cancel out, but they added together in the direction of travel of the light.

Huygens' wavelet model explained various phenomena of light such as refraction and diffraction, but was not attractive to Newton, who stuck to his 'corpuscle' theory. Even so, unlike many of Newton's scientific opponents, Huygens was often in agreement with Newton. The two men met up when Huygens made a visit to England in 1689 and continued to correspond off and on until Huygens died six years later.

Brian Clegg

THE RAINBOW

the 30-second theory

RELATED TOPICS

See also
COLOURS OF THE RAINBOW
page 34

THE SECOND PRISM
page 38

RECOMBINATION
page 42

3-SECOND THRASH

Newton used his understanding of white light's composition, and the way different colours were bent by different amounts when passing through a substance, to explain rainbows.

3-MINUTE THOUGHT

Thirteenth-century proto-scientist Roger Bacon used the rainbow as an example of the importance of experimental science in his great *Opus Majus*. Bacon noted the comparison with the spectra produced by prisms and other shaped pieces of glass and explored how to measure the angle at which a raindrop should be seen to produce a rainbow effect by 'reflection and refraction'. However, he believed that the rainbow colours were an artefact of vision, rather than true colours.

With a clear picture of the way that a prism separated the colours of the spectrum out of white light, Newton was able to go on to describe the mechanism of the most common natural spectrum, the rainbow. Although this had been understood to some degree in the past, it took Newton's explanation of the make-up of white light to truly make sense of it. Newton wrote: 'Why the Colours of the Rainbow appear in falling drops of Rain, is also from [the way white light is composed of the various colours] evident. For, those drops, which refract the Rays, disposed to appear purple, in greatest quantity to the Spectators eye, refract the Rays of other sorts so much less, as to make them pass beside it; and such are the drops in the inside of the Primary Bow, and on the outside of the Second or Exteriour one. So those drops, which refract in greatest plenty the Rays, apt to appear red, toward the Spectators eye, refract those of other sorts so much more, as to make them pass beside it; and such are the drops on the exterior part of the Primary, and interior part of the Secondary Bow.'

3-SECOND BIOGRAPHY
ROGER BACON
1214/20–c.1292
English Franciscan friar who was obsessed with the collection of scientific knowledge

30-SECOND TEXT
Brian Clegg

Different colours in sunlight are refracted differing amounts by the raindrop, breaking up the light to form the rainbow in sky.

THE NATURE OF COLOUR

the 30-second theory

Newton's work with prisms

inspired him to explain why an object appears to be a particular colour. As he put it in a letter to Royal Society secretary Henry Oldenburg, published in February 1672, 'the Colours of all natural Bodies have no other origin than this, that they are variously qualified to reflect one sort of light in greater plenty then another.' So, for instance, when looking at a red object he noted: 'when illustrated with day-light, that is, with all sorts of Rays promiscuously blended, those qualified with red shall abound most in the reflected light, and by their prevalence cause it to appear of that colour.' The white sunlight, as he had demonstrated with his prism experiments, contained every possible colour. If that light then fell on, say, a blue jacket, the colours from red to green would largely would be absorbed, as would a fair amount of light at the indigo/violet end of the spectrum. What was left to be reflected was primarily the blue – and when that light reached his eyes, Newton saw a blue jacket. (We now know that all the light is absorbed, but only light of certain frequencies is re-emitted, with the rest being absorbed as heat.)

RELATED TOPICS
See also
PARTICLES OF LIGHT
page 26

THE RAINBOW
page 34

THE SECOND PRISM
page 38

3-SECOND THRASH
When white light hits an object, some of the colours are absorbed – what is left is reflected and gives the object its apparent colour.

3-MINUTE THOUGHT
Newton realized that while objects have a main apparent colour, they usually reflect other colours to some degree. To demonstrate this he distinguished between 'uncompounded' light of a single spectral colour and 'compounded' light which mixed two or more colours. He pointed out that an object that appeared red in sunlight could in principle take on any colour when illuminated by uncompounded light but it would be muddy and unsatisfactory unless the light contained the colour(s) it reflected 'most copiously'.

3-SECOND BIOGRAPHIES
HENRY OLDENBURG
1619–77
German diplomat and natural philosopher who published Newton's letter to the Royal Society

ROBERT HOOKE
1635–1703
English natural philosopher whose criticisms of Newton's letter started their life-long feud

30-SECOND TEXT
Brian Clegg

A red pepper looks red because light of a predominantly red frequency is re-emitted to the observing eye.

BEYOND PHYSICS

alchemy From the Arabic *al-kimiya*, itself derived from a Greek term for the transmutation of substances to gold and silver, alchemy was the predecessor to chemistry, combining some of the analytical goals of chemistry with the more philosophical pursuit of the 'philosopher's stone' that would turn substances to gold or give eternal life.

Arianism Arianism was the belief of those like Newton who followed the 'Arian heresy'. They thought that the Christian 'Holy Trinity' of Father, Son and Holy Spirit (which is not biblical) did not exist, but rather that there was a single God and that Christ was his ultimate creation. The name comes from the originator of the doctrine, Arius, who lived in Egypt in the third and fourth centuries.

calculus A set of mathematical techniques developed by Newton and Leibniz, calculus has two arms. Differential calculus deals with the way one variable changes with respect to another by looking at the impact of infinitesimally small changes – it might be a rate of change of velocity (acceleration), for instance, or the way that pressure varies with altitude. Integral calculus is the inverse of differential calculus and typically might be used to work out the area under a curve or to add together a collection of increasingly small values. The terminology we use now is that of Leibniz – Newton called it the method of fluxions. Newton and Leibniz developed their ideas separately. Newton probably came up with fluxions first, but Leibniz published on calculus first. The result was a protracted priority dispute.

Antonio Conti Conti was an Italian abbot and mathematician in whom both Newton and Leibniz confided during their dispute over priority on the invention of calculus. Conti acted as something of a go-between.

infinitesimals Particularly small parts of something that are too small to measure. Calculus works by dividing something up smaller and smaller until it has infinitesimally small divisions. As these parts become so small as to effectively vanish away the correct outcome is reached.

Gottfried Leibniz Gottfried Wilhelm Leibniz was a Leipzig-born contemporary of Newton's who was a consummate mathematician, sometimes referred to as the 'continental Newton'. His greatest achievement was the development of calculus and we still use his terminology and symbols, including the long S 'summa' or $(\int)$ representing integration in modern mathematics.

John Locke English philosopher and friend of Newton. Locke was an empiricist – someone who believed that knowledge is not something with which we are born but rather something that comes purely from the input of our senses. This approach emphasizes the importance of evidence above human logic and rhetoric, making it attractive in the move away from the Ancient Greek approach towards modern scientific thinking.

the second prism The central idea of Newton's *experimentum crucis* ('critical experiment'): after light has gone through one prism, forming a rainbow, he separated off a section of colour and passed it again through a second prism, showing that it was bent further (and by different amounts for different colours) but did not change colour further.

theology Literally 'knowledge' or 'an account' of God, theology, sometimes known in academic circles as divinity, was considered the most important academic subject in medieval times, when it was referred to as the 'noblest science'. By Newton's time, as university curricula were revised, it was gradually losing its pre-eminent role.

Two New Sciences Galileo's greatest book, properly *Discorsi e Dimostrazioni Matematiche intorno à due nuoue Scienze Attenenti alla Mecanica & i Movimenti Locali* in the original Italian. The work contains Galileo's ideas on matter and motion and introduces the concept of relativity. It is far more readable today than Newton's books.

MP

the 30-second theory

Newton's story can often seem one in which the greatest upheavals were disputes over scientific priority – it can be easy to forget that he also lived through a tumultuous time in English politics. And for all his reputation as someone who could withdraw completely into a scientific problem, Newton was at the heart of these political changes. When the Roman Catholic James II took over the English throne in 1685, the new monarch was determined to make Catholics at least equal to their Protestant counterparts. At the time, Cambridge University was open only to Protestants and Newton was active amongst those standing up to James and resisting the move to accept Catholics. Newton became one of the university's two members of parliament, representing Cambridge University in the Convention Parliament of 1689 that accepted William of Orange's assumption of the throne to replace James. Admittedly Newton's role as a parliamentarian was not huge – apart from taking part in the momentous vote, his only noted action in the House was a request to have a window closed because there was a draft. Even so, he would also represent Cambridge University for a second term in 1701–02, again with no noticeable impact.

RELATED TOPICS
See also
ROYAL MINT
page 56

NEWTON'S LIBRARY
page 68

3-SECOND BIOGRAPHIES
JAMES II
1633–1701
Second surviving son of
Charles I, reigned 1685–88

WILLIAM OF ORANGE
1650–1702
Dutch prince who reigned
1689–72 as William III of
England, Scotland and Ireland

CHARLES MONTAGU
1661–1715
English nobleman, Chancellor
of the Exchequer 1694–99

MICHAEL FARADAY
1791–1867
English physicist and chemist

30-SECOND TEXT
Brian Clegg

Newton engaged fully with the political upheaval surrounding the deposition of the Roman Catholic James II.

3-SECOND THRASH
Despite Newton's dedication to his academic work, he was prepared to stand up for the Protestant identity of Cambridge University and represented it twice as a member of parliament.

3-MINUTE THOUGHT
It is often said that Isaac Newton was the first person to be knighted for services to science. It is certainly true that until recently it was uncommon for a scientist to receive that honour. (Physicist Michael Faraday, notably, is said to have turned down a knighthood because he did not approve of any honours.) In practice it was Newton's stand in the Protestant cause and his friendship with Charles Montagu, the Chancellor of the Exchequer who appointed him to the Royal Mint, that brought him the knighthood.

ROYAL MINT

the 30-second theory

RELATED TOPIC
See also
MP
page 54

3-SECOND THRASH
Newton spent his later
years working at the
Royal Mint in London,
first as Warden and later
as Master.

Newton's duties as a member of
parliament meant frequent visits to London, and
by the 1690s he had formed a desire to move to
that city on a permanent basis. He let his friends
know he was looking for a suitable position in
the capital. A former student of his named
Charles Montagu had recently become
Chancellor of the Exchequer, and he used his
influence to get his erstwhile professor
appointed to the post of Warden of the Royal
Mint. Newton arrived at the Mint – which at the
time was located inside the Tower of London
– in 1696, and found it in the midst of a crisis.
The country's entire supply of coins was being
reminted, and the project was falling badly
behind schedule. Newton proved a highly
effective administrator – he quickly identified
the bottlenecks where new equipment was
needed, and the project was soon back on track.
With the crisis averted, Newton settled down to
the day-to-day running of the Mint – first as
Warden, later as Master – with the same
ingenuity he had applied to his scientific work.
As his eventual successor John Conduitt put it,
Newton 'had frequent opportunities of
employing his skill in mathematics and
chemistry, particularly in his table of assays
of foreign coins'.

3-MINUTE THOUGHT
Concepts like banknotes
and credit were in their
infancy in Newton's time,
so 'money' was still
virtually synonymous with
coinage. The commonest
form of financial crime was
counterfeiting, and it was
part of Newton's duty as
Warden of the Mint to
track down counterfeiters
and collect evidence
against them. At first he
felt this was beneath him,
but he soon developed a
taste for detective work
– and by all accounts was
extremely successful at it.

3-SECOND BIOGRAPHIES
CHARLES MONTAGU
1661–1715
Close friend of Newton,
Chancellor of the Exchequer
under William III

JOHN CONDUITT
1688–1737
Husband of Newton's niece
who succeeded him as Master
of the Mint

30-SECOND TEXT
Andrew May

*Newton was able to
transfer his keen
mathematical aptitude
and deep knowledge
of chemistry from
academic life to the
busy Royal Mint.*

THE LURE OF ALCHEMY

the 30-second theory

RELATED TOPICS
See also
ALCHEMICAL
EXPERIMENTATION
page 60

NEWTON'S LIBRARY
page 68

3-SECOND THRASH
Newton was a man of his time, believing that there was hidden ancient wisdom to be found – and alchemy, with its mystical connotations, helped shape his approach.

3-MINUTE THOUGHT
Newton was probably the most scientific of any practitioner of operative alchemy, making precise measurements and records of his work. However, his approach to the subject shows a very different approach to that of a modern scientist: he was always searching for symbolic relationships between the spiritual world and the everyday workings of nature. His work on alchemy was long ignored, but it is important to consider it in putting Newton's work and approach into perspective.

It seems strange from a modern viewpoint that a man who is an exemplar of the mould-breaking scientist should have an interest in alchemy, a subject we lump in with astrology as pre-scientific mumbo-jumbo. However, Newton was a man of his time, and saw the world through different eyes. Just as medieval academics built their arguments on theology, the 'noblest of the sciences', so Newton saw his role as revealing the workings of God's creation. Four hundred years earlier, Roger Bacon, the medieval proto-scientist, had described the common belief that the ancients had complete knowledge of how the world worked – knowledge that had now been lost. Newton held the same view. With this in mind, alchemy made more sense and became appealing to a man like Newton. Alchemists concerned themselves with the nature of matter, assuming that all things were composed of the four ancient Greek 'elements' of earth, air, fire and water, which could be broken down and reassembled. Some, like Robert Boyle, would focus mainly on the simple study of how elements combined – speculative alchemy – but with Newton's mystical viewpoint, the appeal was largely operative alchemy, the age-old desire to transmute base metals into gold.

3-SECOND BIOGRAPHIES
ROGER BACON
1214/20–c.1292
English Franciscan friar whose *Opus Majus* gives a good picture of the nature of medieval science

ROBERT BOYLE
1627–91
British pioneer of chemistry who did considerable work in the alchemical tradition.

30-SECOND TEXT
Brian Clegg

The world Newton wanted to understand was, in his eyes, God's creation – and alchemy was one possible path to knowing it.

ALCHEMICAL EXPERIMENTATION

the 30-second theory

The extent of Newton's interest in alchemy, which remained a private pursuit for most of his life, only became clear when the economist John Maynard Keynes bought a collection of his alchemical papers in 1936. We now know that Newton wrote around one million words relating to alchemy and was probably the most widely read man of his time within the area. One notebook in particular details the many chemical experiments Newton conducted over a 30-year period in a shed in the garden attached to his rooms at Trinity College, Cambridge. Due to its effectiveness in refining gold, experiments relating to the chemical element antimony (Sb) featured prominently – in fact, it was antimony's ore, Stibnite Sb_2S_3. Furthermore, in alchemy, certain metals were synonymous with Roman deities. When Newton read Ovid's tale of Vulcan trapping his wife Venus (copper) and her lover Mars (iron) in a metallic net, he saw a method for making this 'net'. This involved extracting antinomy from its ore using iron and then adding copper. This resulted in a crystalline alloy with an apparent network on its surface.

Keynes expanded his collection of Newton's alchemical papers after 1936 and in 1946 bequeathed them to King's College, Cambridge.

NEWTON'S THEOLOGY: ARIANISM

the 30-second theory

RELATED TOPICS
See also
BIBLICAL SCIENCE
page 64
NEWTON'S LIBRARY
page 66

3-SECOND THRASH
Newton believed in a single all-powerful God, and risked accusations of blasphemy by refusing to accept the orthodox doctrine of the Holy Trinity.

3-MINUTE THOUGHT
Newton saw no conflict between science and religious belief. He made this point explicitly in the *General Scholium*, which he appended to the second edition of the *Principia* in 1713. He saw the physical world as clear evidence for the existence of God: 'This most excellently contrived system of the Sun, and planets, and comets, could not have its origin from any other than from the wise conduct and dominion of an intelligent and powerful Being.'

In Newton's time, academic posts often carried religious obligations. When he became a fellow of Trinity College, Cambridge, in 1667, it was on strict condition that he would take Holy Orders – be ordained as a priest – within seven years. This requirement led him to a detailed study of theology, and before long he realized there was at least one fundamental doctrine of the Church of England that he could not accept. Fortunately he managed to secure a special dispensation that relieved him of the obligation to take Holy Orders, but once his interest in theology had been kindled it remained with him for the rest of his life. The doctrine he could not accept was that of the Holy Trinity – that God exists in three persons: Father, Son and Holy Spirit. Instead, Newton believed categorically in a single supreme God. This belief is often referred to as Arianism, after an early Christian heretic named Arius. In Newton's time denial of the Trinity was considered blasphemy, although the view was shared by other prominent thinkers including the philosopher John Locke. Newton expressed his beliefs in a private treatise he sent to Locke in 1690, 'An Historical Account of Two Notable Corruptions of Scripture'. This was eventually published in 1754, almost 30 years after Newton's death.

3-SECOND BIOGRAPHIES
ARIUS
c.250–336
Early Christian priest who opposed the doctrine of the Holy Trinity

JOHN LOCKE
1632–1704
English philosopher and major figure of the Enlightenment

30-SECOND TEXT
Andrew May

Newton was convinced that the creation must be subject 'to the Dominion of One Being ... Supreme Governour of the Universe' – and so could not believe in the Trinity of Father, Son and Holy Ghost.

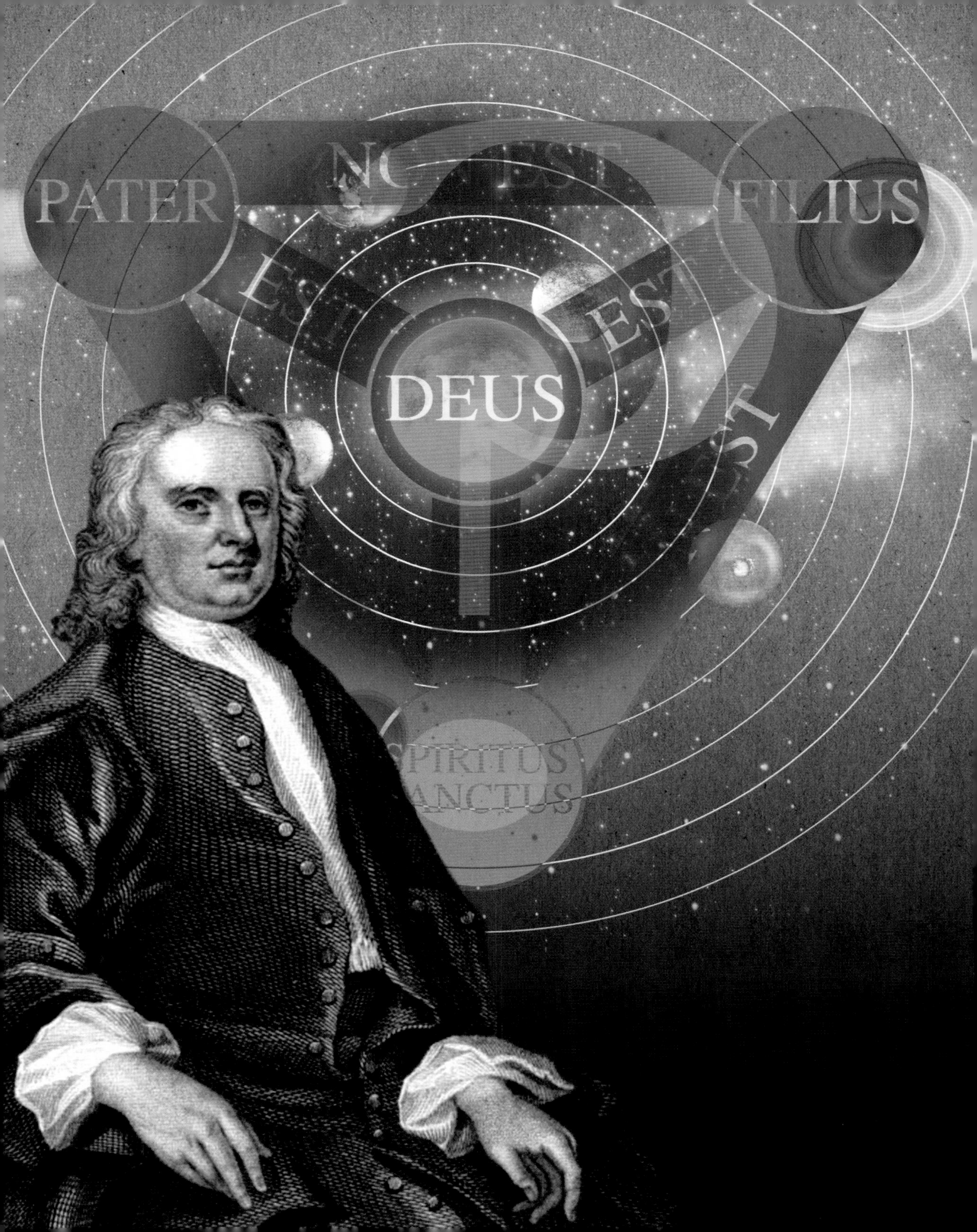
PATER
FILIUS
DEUS
SPIRITUS
SANCTUS
EST
EST
EST
NON EST

BIBLICAL SCIENCE

the 30-second theory

Newton's interest in theology led him to a detailed study of the Bible, which he read not just in Latin and English translations but also in the original Hebrew and Greek. He was particularly fascinated by the chronology of the ancient world, as revealed in the Old Testament and other writings. He became convinced that the generally accepted timeline of events was wrong, and developed his own alternative version. In 1716 this came to the attention of the Italian philosopher Antonio Conti, who in turn mentioned it to the Princess of Wales, Caroline of Brandenburg-Ansbach. Feeling that his chronology was not yet ready for publication, Newton lent a copy to the princess on the understanding it was for her eyes only. Conti, however, subsequently took the manuscript to France where an unauthorized version was published. Newton's last letter to the *Philosophical Transactions of the Royal Society*, in May 1725, was an attempt to distance himself from the chronology that had been published under his name in France. His final version, with which he was much happier, was published a year after his death as *The Chronology of Ancient Kingdoms Amended*. It is a huge work, which demonstrates Newton's careful research and attention to detail, but sadly there is little in it that has stood the test of time.

RELATED TOPICS
See also
NEWTON'S THEOLOGY:
ARIANISM
page 62

NEWTON'S LIBRARY
page 68

3-SECOND BIOGRAPHIES
ANTONIO CONTI
1677–1749
Italian philosopher

CAROLINE OF
BRANDENBURG-ANSBACH
1683–1737
Princess of Wales 1714–27,
wife of King George II (reigned
from 1727)

30-SECOND TEXT
Andrew May

3-SECOND THRASH
Newton was fascinated by the timeline of events portrayed in the Bible, and put enormous effort into producing a detailed chronology of the ancient world.

3-MINUTE THOUGHT
As well as the chronology of the past, Newton was also interested in what the Bible had to say about the future. Based on his reading of the *Book of Daniel*, he calculated that Christ's Second Coming, which many of his contemporaries believed was imminent, would take place no earlier than 2060. For Newton this lay in the distant future; it seems much closer today!

Newton's **Observations upon the Prophecies of Daniel and the Apocalypse of St John** *was published in 1733. He calculated Christ's Second Coming as due in 2060.*

1 July 1646
Born in Leipzig, Saxony

1662
Receives BA in philosophy at Leipzig University

1666
Receives doctorate in law from the University of Altdorf

1672
Begins four years in Paris

1673
Elected fellow of the Royal Society

1675
Joins French Academy of Sciences as an honorary member

1676
Moves to Hanover as counsellor

1677
Becomes Privy Counsellor of Justice

1677
Proposes a European federation of states

1684
Publishes *Nova methodus pro maximis et minimis* ('New Method for Maximums and Minimums'), outlining calculus

1700
Helps set up the Berlin Academy of Sciences

1710
Publishes his philosophical treatise, *Théodicée*

1713
The Royal Society's priority report (written by Newton) finds in favour of Newton

14 November 1716
Dies in Hanover

GOTTFRIED LEIBNIZ

Though Newton had many arguments in his academic life, the one with the biggest impact was probably his long-running priority debate with Gottfried Wilhelm von Leibniz over the invention of calculus. (Or just Leibniz. He used the noble 'von' form, but his right to it is disputed.)

Born into an academic family in Leipzig in 1646, from an early age Leibniz paralleled Newton in questioning the prevalent dependence at the time on ancient Greek natural philosophy. At university he initially studied philosophy and law, but discovered an increasing interest in mathematics, which became central to his work as he moved away from Leipzig.

In 1672, Leibniz was sidetracked for four years on a diplomatic mission to Paris, but this enabled him to make excellent contacts in the mathematical and scientific world; he became a Fellow of the Royal Society in 1673 (the year after Newton). He also demonstrated to the Society a mechanical calculator he had designed. It was while in Paris, in 1676, that he wrote his treatise *De quadratura arithmetica circuli ellipseos et hyperbolae cujus corollarium est trigonometria sine tabulis* ('On the Arithmetical Quadrature of Circles, Ellipses and the Hyperbolae'). This was primarily on indivisibles, what we would now call infinitesimals, an essential component of calculus. The treatise shows how Leibniz's thinking was developing at this time, but it would not influence others, because, remarkably, it was not published until 1993.

Leibniz developed this theory further, corresponding with Henry Oldenburg and John Collins in London, both of whom were partially familiar with Newton's ideas. Newton sent a couple of letters to Leibniz, seemingly attempting to establish his precedence, but Leibniz went ahead and published his version of calculus, including the notation that we still use, in 1684, well before Newton. Veiled accusations of plagiarism were brought into the open in a paper by Scottish mathematician John Keill that explicitly accused Leibniz of stealing Newton's ideas.

The dispute rumbled on for years, opening a rift between British and continental European mathematicians that would take 100 years to heal. Leibniz continued to work to the end of his life in both mathematics and philosophy, where he made significant advances in formal logic, but nothing else he did would have the lasting impact of his calculus.

Brian Clegg

NEWTON'S LIBRARY

the 30-second theory

Newton accumulated an unusually large library at a time when books were both expensive and relatively rare. When he died he left behind around 2,100 titles, many of them well thumbed and dog-eared, as Newton seems to have frequently turned the page corners both to mark places and to pull together sections of text. The library was virtually intact until 1920, when a good half of the books were auctioned off. Some of the volumes were inscribed with details of how Newton obtained them, and in some – about 30 – he wrote the price, which ranged from 1s 6d to £7. That's around £900 now in pure monetary value, or closer to £14,000 in the price of labour. What's most surprising is the balance of contents of the books. Only 109 covered physics and astronomy, with 138 on alchemy, 126 on maths and a massive 477 on theology. (To be fair, some of the 'maths' books covered physics, including Newton's own *Principia*.) Amongst the many other topics were 46 travel books, 149 works of classical literature and 58 modern, 31 on economics and 6 on medals. Though this was certainly a working library it had some surprising omissions such as Galileo's key physics book *Two New Sciences*.

RELATED TOPICS
See also
THE ROYAL SOCIETY
page 18

ALCHEMICAL
EXPERIMENTATION
page 60

BIBLICAL SCIENCE
page 64

3-SECOND BIOGRAPHIES
GALILEO GALILEI
1564–1642
Italian natural philosopher

SIR JOHN KEDERMISTER
d.1631
Benefactor of the Kedermister Library in Langley Marish church.

30-SECOND TEXT
Brian Clegg

3-SECOND THRASH
Newton's library gives an insight into the wide range of his interests: less than one-third of the books were on maths and science.

3-MINUTE THOUGHT
A useful way of putting Newton's library into context is to compare it with an extant personal library of the period, the Kedermister Library, which is housed in the church of St Mary, in Langley Marish in Berkshire. Founded in 1631 for the "ministers of ... Langley and such others of the County of Buckingham as resort thereto", its contemporary catalogue lists 307 books, mostly religious but also including a herbal. The library of Trinity College, Cambridge, by comparison, held 3,000–4,000 books at this time.

When Newton died in 1727 his voluminous library was sold off to John Huggins, warden of the Fleet Prison in London, for £300.

$$F = \frac{GM_1 M_2}{r^2}$$

CALCULUS

acceleration Unlike in normal usage, in physics acceleration means any change of velocity (so 'deceleration' is just a negative acceleration). Because velocity involves both speed and direction, if something changes direction while maintaining a constant speed it is still undergoing acceleration. Quantitatively, acceleration is a measure of the rate of change of velocity.

Bishop Berkeley's *The Analyst* With the striking subtitle *A Discourse Addressed to an Infidel Mathematician*, this is a short book written by Bishop George Berkeley criticizing the basis for the method of fluxions and calculus. Although the intention seems to have been largely to redress a religious offence caused by Newton's supporter Edmund Halley, Berkeley makes the important mathematical point that the original method appeared to involve equations in which zero was divided by zero, which should be mathematically indeterminate.

Augustin-Louis Cauchy Cauchy was a 19th-century mathematician who made Newton and Leibniz's versions of calculus more robust by replacing infinity and zero with variable values that tended to infinity or zero, but never went all the way.

continual flowing motion Newton was aware of the problems that arose from the way that his method of fluxions dealt with infinitesimal quantities that vanished away to nothing. He tried to get around this by saying that he was dealing with continually flowing motion, hence his use of terms of flow like fluent and fluxion. Newton's attempt was smoke and mirrors; the problem was real and would not be addressed for several hundred years.

differential calculus The name given by Leibniz to what Newton called the method of fluxions; still the term used today. Differential calculus is used to discover the rate at which one value changes with respect to another value by examining the effect of infinitesimally small changes, and then allowing those small changes to tend to zero.

fluxional calculus Newton's version of calculus in which the rate of change of values called fluents was measured in terms of fluxions, for what we now call differential calculus, and reversed to produce the fluents in what we now call integral calculus.

fluxions In Newton's version of differential calculus, the method of fluxions, a fluxion was the rate at which something changed. It was denoted by a dot over the letter representing the value, so-called 'pricked notation', so an x with a dot over it meant the rate of change of x with time, which would be presented as dx/dt in modern calculus.

infinitesimal quantities Particularly small parts of something that are too small to measure. Calculus works by dividing something up smaller and smaller until it is divided up into infinitesimally small quantities. As these parts become so small as to effectively vanish away, the correct outcome is reached.

integral calculus The inverse of differential calculus, and the term used by Leibniz and still in use today. Integral calculus is used to, for instance, find the area under a curve by adding up the areas of small slices of the shape, which are made thinner and thinner until their width tends to zero.

log-line A knotted length of rope with a board on the end, also called a chip log (or just a log), dropped behind a ship to measure its speed as the line unreeled, hence the nautical unit of speed, the knot.

maxima and minima points The points on a curve that have largest (maxima) and smallest (minima) values.

summa In Latin, *summa* is just a sum, but Leibniz used the term as a special case of the limit of the sum of, for instance, a collection of slices of the area under a curve, as the thickness of those slices gets thinner and thinner. He represented 'summa' by an elongated S, which we now call the integral sign ($\int$).

THE ACCELERATION PROBLEM

the 30-second theory

RELATED TOPICS

See also
FLUXIONS
page 76

PLANETARY MOTION
page 136

From the moment we open our eyes to see the morning alarm clock to our drive home from work or school, we are constantly using tools to measure time and space. But in Newton's England mechanical clocks were still a rarity and a unit to measure speed was only just becoming mainstream. The term 'knot' was based on a sailor's crude technique of dropping a 'log-line' into the water to work out a ship's speed, which was given by the ratio of the length of rope and time. This can be represented graphically: a plot of distance as a function of time looks like a straight line whose slope is speed. But what if the speed changes, so a motion is represented by a curve? To a society only just adopting a terminology for speed and lacking precise tools for measuring it, this was difficult territory. Newton studied and developed the mathematics of ellipses and curves mapped out by French mathematician René Descartes and applied this to motion, seeking the slope of a curve at any point – the rate of change or acceleration. Mathematics could not yet make sense of the orbits of the planets, but Newton's method would give him new powers to describe motion accurately.

3-SECOND THRASH
Mathematics lacked the tools to describe motion in terms of rates of change – or acceleration. Newton tackled this limitation as a geometrical problem.

3-MINUTE THOUGHT
The log-line or chip log was the first speedometer – knots were tied at intervals 15.24 m (50 ft) or 8 fathoms (14.6 ms or 48 ft), and a sailor would count how many knots passed through his fingers over 30 or 28.8 seconds, measured using a sand-timer. The number of knots in that period would be the speed in knots or nautical miles per hour.

3-SECOND BIOGRAPHIES
RENÉ DESCARTES
1596–1650
French mathematician who used algebra to describe geometry

ISAAC BARROW
1630–77
English mathematician who lectured on geometry and optics at Cambridge University

30-SECOND TEXT
Sophie Hebden

If the speed is not changing at a steady rate the result is acceleration in the form of a curve.

FLUXIONS

the 30-second theory

Newton started to think about the nature of acceleration, and mathematical approaches to describing it, during an enforced stay at Woolsthorpe when Cambridge University was closed down due to the plague between 1665 and 1667. But it would be an exaggeration to say that he developed his method of fluxions at the time. This is what we would call differential calculus – integral calculus was then known as fluents. It would take a number of years for the full method to be established, and his book, *The Method of Fluxions*, which was published posthumously in 1736, was first sketched out in the early 1670s. Aware of the dangers of dealing with infinitesimally small numbers, which came back to haunt him in Bishop Berkeley's *The Analyst*, Newton tried to base his approach on the concept of continual flowing motion, hence his terms suggestive of flow and change. He called the rate at which something changed a 'fluxion', while the resultant change was known as a 'fluent'. The fluxion that Newton would represent as an *x* with a dot over it, is the same as what we would now call dx/dt in the modern notation of calculus, representing the rate of change of *x* with time.

RELATED TOPICS
See also
THE ACCELERATION PROBLEM
page 74

TWO NOTATIONS
page 78

3-SECOND BIOGRAPHY
GEORGE BERKELEY
1685–1753
Anglo-Irish philosopher bishop

30-SECOND TEXT
Brian Clegg

3-SECOND THRASH
Between 1666 and the early 1670s, Newton developed his method of fluxions, what we would now call differential calculus, reflecting the ratio of two infinitesimal changes.

3-MINUTE THOUGHT
Newton hoped that by only representing the *ratios* of changes – dotted *x* was inseparably a ratio – rather than individual vanishingly small values, he could avoid the dangers of infinitesimals. The final result was produced by the 'ultimate ratio of change', which was the ratio of the tiny changes in, say, distance and time, at the moment that they vanished away. His fluxion was the value 'with which the body moved … at the very instant when it arrives' at a point.

Newton thought of nonstop flowing motion – like that of a stream. He devised his 'pricked notation' to represent the ratio of change.

TWO NOTATIONS

the 30-second theory

While there seems no doubt that
Newton did develop his method of fluxions
independently of Leibniz's calculus, and it was
widely used in England for 100 years, anyone
who has studied calculus at school would find it
baffling. When Leibniz developed his version of
the same method, he used a totally different
notation, calling his method 'calculus', as we
now know it. We have kept Leibniz's notation
for a good reason – because it was better.
Newton had developed his notation conscious
of the dangers of appearing to work with
individual infinitesimal values, and so forces his
fluxions always to be ratios by using x with a dot
over it (called by Newton 'pricked notation') to
represent the rate of change of x. Two dots
would be used to mark what is now called the
second derivative – the rate of change of the
rate of change. In Leibniz's notation these are
dx/dt and $d2x/dt2$ respectively, explicitly
bringing in the infinitesimal changes in the value
of x and time. This then extends easily to dx/dy
for dealing with the way x changes with y,
where Newton had to effectively use a ratio of
ratios with dotted x over dotted y.

RELATED TOPICS
See also
THE ACCELERATION PROBLEM
page 74

FLUXIONS
page 76

THE GREAT PRIORITY DISPUTE
page 84

3-SECOND BIOGRAPHY
GOTTFRIED WILHELM LEIBNIZ
1646–1716
German mathematician, one of
Newton's greatest opponents

30-SECOND TEXT
Brian Clegg

3-SECOND THRASH
Both Newton and Leibniz
developed notation to
represent the functions
of calculus, but those
produced by Leibniz
were more practical and
Newton's were gradually
phased out.

3-MINUTE THOUGHT
Another benefit of the
Leibniz notation was
the use of the flexible ∫
symbol to represent what
Leibniz called integration
– the inverse of the
differentiation used
to calculate changes.
Integration, which
deals with combining
infinitesimal shapes or
numbers to work out, say,
the area under a curve, is
represented by this
extended S, a symbol for
summa, where Newton
called this the method of
fluents, represented by a
vertical bar over the value
to be integrated.

*Despite a small amount
of communication
between them, Leibniz
and Newton seem to
have developed
calculus independently.
But Newton thought he
had been plagiarized.*

12 March 1685
Born at Dysart Castle, Ireland

1707
Receives Masters from Trinity College, Dublin

1707
Publishes mathematical studies *Arithmetica* and *Miscellanea mathmatica*

1709
Publishes *An Essay Towards a New Theory of Vision*

1710
Publishes *Treatise Concerning the Principles of Human Knowledge*

1721
Ordained into the Church of Ireland

1722
Becomes Dean of Dromore

1724
Becomes Dean of Derry

1725
Begins work on the Bermuda College project

1728
Marries Anne Forster

1729
Travels to Rhode Island

1732
Returns to London

1730s
Involved in the forming of the Foundling Hospital, and one of its first governors

1734
Ordained Bishop of Cloyne

1734
Publishes *The Analyst*

1752
Retires and moves to Oxford, where his son lives

14 January 1753
Dies in Oxford

GEORGE BERKELEY

Bishop George Berkeley's greatest claim to fame may be his assessment of whether a tree truly existed if it was hidden in the middle of a forest and no one was aware of it. He pointed out that since God was everywhere and knew everything, someone was aware of it – so the tree definitely existed. But in Newton's story, Berkeley is better known for publishing a stinging attack on the method of fluxions and calculus in general.

Berkeley was born in Dysart Castle, outside Thomastown in Ireland, son of a gentleman farmer. His family were recent immigrants, having left England for political reasons after the Restoration of the English monarchy in 1660. He was educated at Trinity College, Dublin, and was ordained into the Anglican Church of Ireland. He was, however, no stuffy unworldly clergyman. He was already well established (if controversial) in philosophical circles before his ordination and published some original thinking on vision, reflecting his views on the nature of matter.

Berkeley travelled to Newport, Rhode Island, where he spent three years working on a project to build a college on Bermuda. The project failed, but on his return it left him in good social standing. His stories made him popular with the queen, which resulted in an unexpected appointment to a bishopric. The queen had suggested Berkeley be put forward for the affluent position of the Dean of Down in Ireland. But it was thought that the Lord Lieutenant of Ireland would be offended by this influence from on high, and the request was ignored. In a biography of Berkeley from 1776 it is noted that the queen responded that if they wouldn't let Berkeley 'be a *Dean* in Ireland, he should be a Bishop'. (This was odd, as he already held a different deanery.) Berkeley was made Bishop of Cloyne instead.

It was from Cloyne that Berkeley entered the fray over calculus. He had a personal dislike of Edmund Halley and responded to Halley's promotion of Newton's work with the scathing attack *The Analyst: A Discourse Addressed to an Infidel Mathematician*. Despite religious provocation from the atheist Halley, Berkeley was a reasonable mathematician and made genuine complaints about the cavalier way that early calculus dealt with infinitesimals. While Berkeley's philosophy had little long-term impact, there was no doubt that his contribution to the debate over calculus had an impact on the development of mathematics in the following decades.

Brian Clegg

NEWTON'S SECRET MISSIVE

the 30-second theory

Newton developed his fluxional calculus in the mid-1660s, but he didn't explicitly disclose it for many decades. Gottfried Leibniz, who was studying under Christiaan Huygens in Paris, visited London for two months in 1673. At the Royal Society he met some of Newton's close acquaintances, including Henry Oldenburg, and afterwards continued to correspond with them. Huygens had not yet met Newton, who was unpublished at the time, but he gained the impression that he was expert at series – a mathematical technique for adding up sequences of numbers. By 1675 Leibniz had developed his own differential calculus, and in June 1676 Oldenburg passed him a letter from Newton describing his work on series. It makes no mention of calculus. Leibniz immediately replied to Newton, via Oldenburg, asking for clarifications and describing his own work on series. Newton responded in October 1676 that he had developed a general method of drawing tangents to curves and of finding their maxima and minima points, but did not wish to disclose the details. He hid his fluxions and fluents by writing: "5accdae10effh11i4l3m9n6oq qr8sllt9v3x: llab3cddloeaeegloillrm7n6o3p3q6r 5sllt8vx, 3acae4egh5i4l4m5n8oq4r3s6t4vaadda eeeeee-iijmmnnooprrsssstttuu." And he noted down the meaning in his jottings book.

RELATED TOPICS
See also
FLUXIONS
page 76

TWO NOTATIONS
page 78

THE GREAT PRIORITY DISPUTE
page 84

3-SECOND THRASH
Newton delayed publishing his fluxional calculus for decades, only alluding to it in correspondence with German mathematician Gottfried Leibniz ten years later, hiding its mention in secret code.

3-MINUTE THOUGHT
In the 17th century scientific reputation wasn't earned by publishing papers in scientific journals; instead the focus was on gaining patronage from royalty. Strange through Newton's behaviour seems today, it was not unusual to hide an intellectual discovery from a third party by writing it in code, or, as in this case, a frequency count of letters in a sentence.

3-SECOND BIOGRAPHIES
HENRY OLDENBURG
1619–77
German theologian and scientist, first secretary to the Royal Society

CHRISTIAAN HUYGENS
1629–95
Dutch natural philosopher who had many disagreements with Newton

GOTTFRIED WILHELM LEIBNIZ
1646–1716
German mathematician who published his work on calculus before Newton

30-SECOND TEXT
Sophie Hebden

Newton noted the meaning of his secret statement on fluxions and fluents.

"5accdac10cffhIIi4l3m9n6oqqr8sIIt9v3x:

IIab3cddIocacgIoillrm7n6o3p3q6r 5sIIt8vx,

3acac4cgh5i4I4m5n8oq4r3s6t4

vaaddaccccccciijmmnnnooprrsssssttuu."

THE GREAT PRIORITY DISPUTE

the 30-second theory

Leibniz published his first papers on calculus in 1684 and 1686, but made no mention of Newton's methods using series. When Newton finally published a pair of mathematical papers laying out his method of fluxions in 1704, he claimed priority for its discovery. His techniques were effectively the same as Leibniz's differential calculus, but with different notation – sparking one of the fiercest priority disputes in scientific history. Newton had a number of complaints against Leibniz, but the most significant focused on a letter Newton had sent to John Collins at the Royal Society in 1672, in which he described fluxions completely, and which Leibniz was shown when he visited London in 1676. But Leibniz had already invented calculus independently himself by then, and historical analysis indicates he was more interested in other details in the letter. As the importance of the discovery of calculus unfolded, more people joined the fray. The Royal Society launched an enquiry, but it was far from neutral: Newton himself secretly authored and reviewed it. Leibniz died in 1716 before anything was settled, and the dispute continued for many years, hindering mathematical progress in England where loyalty to Newton's notation became a matter of national pride.

RELATED TOPICS
See also
FLUXIONS
page 76

TWO NOTATIONS
page 78

A DISCOURSE ADDRESSED TO AN INFIDEL MATHEMATICIAN
page 86

3-SECOND BIOGRAPHIES
JOHN COLLINS
1625–83
English mathematician and fellow of the Royal Society

GOTTFRIED WILHELM LEIBNIZ
1646–1716
German mathematician and philosopher, member of the Berlin Academy of Sciences

30-SECOND TEXT
Sophie Hebden

3-SECOND THRASH
Today we credit both Newton and Leibniz with the discovery of calculus, but they would not acknowledge that they created it independently; instead each accused the other of plagiarism.

3-MINUTE THOUGHT
Newton's secrecy early on in his career lay behind the dispute – had he made his fluxional calculus public from the start for the world to use, the dispute would not have happened. Yet he had intentionally kept the method to himself – for example, converting the mathematical working in his *Principia* from its original form using fluxions to a considerably less obvious approach that relied primarily on geometry. But once Leibniz published there was no going back.

Newton won the priority dispute at the time, but sadly the two scientists' quarrel held back progress.

$$F(x) = f(x)$$

$$\int f(x)\,dx = F(x)$$

A DISCOURSE ADDRESSED TO AN INFIDEL MATHEMATICIAN

the 30-second theory

The philosopher Bishop George

Berkeley wrote a pamphlet entitled *The Analyst: A Discourse Addressed to an Infidel Mathematician*, in which he attacked the basis for Newton's fluxions (and Leibniz's calculus). The infidel in question was probably Edmund Halley, the Astronomer Royal, who had been Newton's staunchest supporter for many years. Unusually for the time, Halley was an atheist and had persuaded a friend of Berkeley's to recant his faith on his deathbed. Berkeley took revenge by unpicking the heart of the method of fluxions, central to the masterpiece of Halley's protégé. The bishop pointed out that the method involved working with inconceivably small quantities – ones that could still be used in mathematics and yet were assumed to have become so small that they disappeared. Berkeley ironically referred to these with a neat turn of phrase as 'the ghosts of departed quantities'. This didn't seem to make sense – yet it worked. All the users of the method of fluxions could do was take it on faith. Berkeley criticized both the approach and Halley's attacks on the reliance on faith in religion, which seemed hypocritical.

RELATED TOPICS
See also
FLUXIONS
page 76

THE GREAT PRIORITY DISPUTE
page 84

FIXING CALCULUS
page 88

3-SECOND BIOGRAPHIES
EDMUND HALLEY
1656–1742
English astronomer and second Astronomer Royal

GEORGE BERKELEY
1685–1753
Anglo-Irish philosopher bishop who challenged the basis of fluxions and calculus

30-SECOND TEXT
Brian Clegg

3-SECOND THRASH
Bishop Berkeley argued that fluxions were flawed because they involved performing arithmetic, including division, on non-existent values.

3-MINUTE THOUGHT
The attack from Berkeley was not mere religious backbiting. Although the method of fluxions produced the right answer, the way it worked was dubious. When these 'ghosts of departed quantities' were set to zero, the result was an equation where zero was divided by zero. This is a mathematical disaster. A fraction with zero on top is zero, and zero on the bottom is infinite. Divide zero by zero and the result is impossible to determine.

In Berkeley's eyes, faith underpinned the method of calculus a much as it did his own religious life as a Christian.

22	23	43	63
3	24	44	64
4		45	65
5		46	66
6	27	47	67
7	28		
8	29	49	69
	30	50	70
	31		71
			72
	33	53	73
14	34	54	74
15	35	55	75
16	36	56	76
17	37	57	77
18	38	58	78
19	39	59	79
20	40	60	80
21	41	61	81

FIXING CALCULUS

the 30-second theory

3-SECOND THRASH
Calculus was mathematically flawed because it allowed infinitesimals to become zero – even so, it worked. Later mathematicians rescued the process by not requiring zero to be reached.

3-MINUTE THOUGHT
Although Cauchy's approach was sufficient for practical purposes, in the 1850s Karl Weierstrass improved the approach mathematically by bringing in the concept of limits. In effect what Weierstrass did was to take the infinity out of calculus (even though the symbol still crops up in integration) by providing a mechanism that makes it possible to establish that a result is heading for a limit if the result approaches that limit faster than a required minimum.

Newton tried to use ratios to hide away risky mathematical operations like dividing by infinitesimal quantities. But his method of fluxions was not mathematically secure because it allowed those infinitesimal quantities to become zero – resulting in operations like dividing zero by zero. George Berkeley was correct in highlighting that this was the case. Newton doesn't seem to have worried unduly because the approach produced the right results, enabling him to undertake his work on forces and gravity. But later mathematicians realized that this was an unsustainable position – and Newton's other attempt to patch things up pointed the direction for those mathematicians to take. Rather than have his fluxion, represented by a squashed letter o, become zero, he merely required it to 'tend to zero'. So when starting with something like $2x + o$, he would not set o to zero to obtain the result $2x$, but would rather say that the result 'tends to $2x$ as o tends to o'. Newton's sleight of hand was formalized in the 1820s by Augustin-Louis Cauchy, who suggested that both infinity and infinitesimal quantities were variable: they were not a fixed number, but rather a label for something that approached infinity or zero but never actually reached it.

RELATED TOPICS
See also
FLUXIONS
page 76

TWO NOTATIONS
page 78

A DISCOURSE ADDRESSED TO AN INFIDEL MATHEMATICIAN
page 86

3-SECOND BIOGRAPHIES
AUGUSTIN-LOUIS CAUCHY
1789–1857
French mathematician who formalized Newton's idea of 'tending to' a value

KARL WEIERSTRASS
1815–97
German mathematician who introduced the concept of limits to remove infinities from calculus

30-SECOND TEXT
Brian Clegg

You cannot solve o/o. Newton and his successors defined very big or very tiny quantities as tending towards infinity or zero but never reaching it.

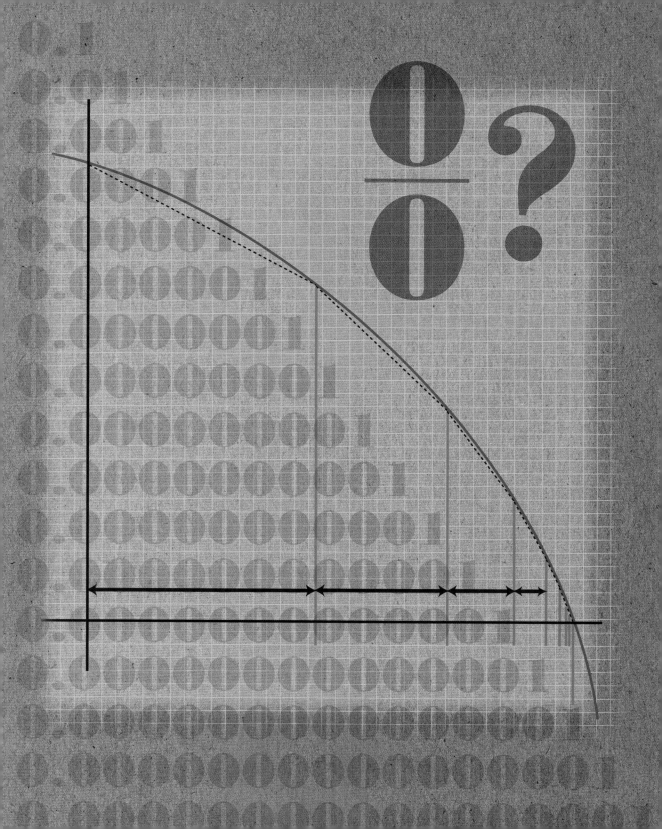

THE PHYSICS OF MOTION

THE PHYSICS OF MOTION
GLOSSARY

absolute motion The assumption that there is some definitive position in comparison to which all motion can be measured. Originally this definitive position was the Earth, but Galileo made it clear that there was no special location (and Einstein would do even more with this).

centrifugal force Although a centripetal force is applied, someone in a car that is turning feels an apparent force outwards. This is just inertia trying to keep the person travelling in a straight line – the actual force is centripetal force, pulling inwards away from that straight line. But that apparent, outwards force is called centrifugal force.

centripetal force A concept defined by Newton, centripetal force builds on his first law of motion. The first law says that unless a force is applied, a moving body will travel in a straight line. So when, for instance, a planet orbits a star, there must be a force towards the star that is pulling the planet out of its straight-line path. This force, towards the centre of motion, is a centripetal force.

gravitational mass The property of matter that makes it attract other matter. The greater the gravitational mass, the greater the force with which a body will attract another body. Gravitational mass appears to be identical to inertial mass, although it need not have been.

inertial mass The property of matter that makes it difficult to change its state of motion. The more inertial mass it has, the more force it takes to start it moving or to slow it down when it is moving. Inertial mass appears to be identical to gravitational mass, though it need not have been.

law of inertia Another name for Newton's first law of motion.

Newton's first law of motion Also called the law of inertia. The first law says that a body will stay at rest or in uniform motion in a straight line (that is, with a fixed velocity) unless a force acts on it.

Newton's second law of motion Originally in the form that a change of motion is proportional to the force applied and takes place in the direction of the application of force, it is now simply stated as $F=ma$, where F is the force applied, m is the mass of the object the force is applied to and a is the resultant acceleration – the rate of change of the object's velocity.

Newton's third law of motion Usually stated as: 'Every action has an equal and opposite reaction.' The result is that if you push something, it pushes back on you, as demonstrated in the recoil of a gun or a rocket motor in flight, where a force backwards on the fuel produces an opposite force forwards on the rocket.

Principia Newton's masterpiece, *Philosophiæ Naturalis Principia Mathematica* ('Mathematical Principles of Natural Philosophy') as it is more properly known, gave us his three laws of motion and his law of universal gravitation, showing that the same principle is responsible for an apple falling and for planets orbiting the Sun. The book was published in 1687 in Latin and was deliberately made less than easy to read, as Newton wanted to limit its audience to experienced natural philosophers.

relative motion Galileo introduced the concept of relativity – that absolute motion is meaningless, and what is important is relative motion. Relative motion is our velocity with respect to a chosen observer. So, for instance, standing in a plane, I might have a relative motion of 700 km/h (435 mph) compared to the ground, but zero compared to another passenger.

weight We are used to weight being a measure of how much stuff there is in something, but the correct scientific measure of this is mass. Weight tells us the force given to that mass by gravity. On the surface of the Earth, the two are the same; in space, however, mass remains the same but an object has no weight.

MASS VERSUS WEIGHT

the 30-second theory

Right at the start of his masterpiece, the *Principia*, Newton makes a few definitions – some of new ideas and others of existing concepts, making their meaning clear. The first definition is 'quantity of matter', which Newton gives the new name 'mass'. He makes it clear that this is related to a body's weight, telling us that 'by making very accurate experiments with pendulums I have found it be proportional to weight'. Newton spent some time inching towards this concept, in an earlier draft referring to 'the quantity or amount of matter being moved, apart from the considerations of gravity'. Mass, then, was a fundamental characteristic of matter, whereas weight was the result of the interaction of that mass with another mass due to their gravitational attraction. A body floating in space has mass, but is weightless. It has been argued that Galileo could never have matched Newton's achievements because he only ever worked with the concept of weight. In modern relativistic physics, Newton's observation that mass is proportional to weight is equivalent to the observation that inertial mass (the property in Newton's laws of motion) and gravitational mass (the property in the law of gravity) are proportional.

RELATED TOPICS
See also
THE FIRST LAW OF MOTION
page 96

THE SECOND LAW OF MOTION
page 98

THE INVERSE SQUARE LAW
page 128

3-SECOND BIOGRAPHIES
GALILEO GALILEI
1564–1642
Italian natural philosopher who took major steps in explaining mechanics and motion

JEAN RICHER
1630–96
French astronomer who performed experiments with pendulums

EDMUND HALLEY
1656–1742
English astronomer who made observations on St Helena

30-SECOND TEXT
Brian Clegg

An astronaut in space has mass but is weightless, whereas on Earth the effects of gravity will give the astronaut weight.

3-SECOND THRASH
Newton moved from the measure of weight, which reflects the force of gravity in a location, to mass, which is only a property of the matter present.

3-MINUTE THOUGHT
One of the reasons why Newton could distinguish between mass and weight without venturing into space is that adventurous astronomers (notably Jean Richer and Edmund Halley) discovered that the weight of an object was subtly different in a distant location. Pendulums, for example, exhibited variations in their period – Newton argued that the mass of the pendulum bob did not influence its period, but its weight did, as a variation in weight reflected a change in the force of gravity.

THE FIRST
LAW OF MOTION

the 30-second theory

Having defined mass in *Principia*, Newton then states his 'axioms' or 'laws of motion'. His first law is often called the law of inertia, which he defined thus: 'Every body perseveres in its state of rest, or of uniform motion in a right line, unless it is compelled to change that state by forces impressed thereon.' It's pretty obvious that stationary objects remain stationary unless a net force acts on them. But the converse is also true: if an object is moving at a constant speed it will remain moving at a constant speed in a straight line unless a force acts on it. The law is less intuitive for moving objects because we are accustomed to dealing with friction – a force that slows and stops motion. But in some situations you can get rid of the majority of friction. Think of how a hockey puck moves across an air hockey table. The puck keeps moving at a constant speed until it bounces off the side of the table; without any friction at all it would continue moving forever. Newton recognized that in space, where there is no friction from air, planets and comets 'persevere their motions … for a much longer time'.

RELATED TOPICS
See also
MASS VERSUS WEIGHT
page 94

INERTIA
page 104

3-SECOND BIOGRAPHIES
RENÉ DESCARTES
1596–1650
French philosopher who defined his own set of three laws concerning motion

EDMUND HALLEY
1656–1742
English astronomer who printed the first 60 copies of *Principia* at his own expense.

30-SECOND TEXT
Sophie Hebden

3-SECOND THRASH
If there is no overall force acting on an object, it will move at a constant velocity or remain at rest if it is at rest.

3-MINUTE THOUGHT
Critical to Newton's first law is the idea of a net or overall force acting on a body. If the forces acting on a body – including those due to gravity – are balanced, the body moves at a constant velocity or remains at rest if it is stationary. In seeking to explain the orbital motion of the planets, Newton first had to define how force affects an object's motion due to inertia.

If friction is reduced, an object will carry on moving for a very long time – forever, if there is no friction at all.

THE SECOND
LAW OF MOTION

the 30-second theory

Although Newton's second law is subtly hidden when it comes to gravity, it is still present in practically every situation where an object is accelerated. In its original form it tells us that 'A change in motion is proportional to the motive force impressed and takes place along the straight line in which that force is impressed.' Before stating his laws, Newton gave a number of definitions, and the quantity of motion he has in mind 'arises from the velocity and the quantity of matter jointly' – it was what we would now call its momentum, made up of mass multiplied by velocity. Newton was saying that the change in momentum is proportional to the change in the force applied, so 'If some force generates any motion, twice the force will generate twice the motion.' What Newton had in mind was an 'impulsive force' – like giving something a kick – rather than a continually acting force, which he elsewhere made clear would produce the more familiar form of the second law dealing with a continuously applied force, that force = mass x acceleration.

RELATED TOPICS
See also
THE FIRST LAW OF MOTION
page 96

THE THIRD LAW OF MOTION
page 100

INERTIA
page 104

3-SECOND BIOGRAPHIES
GALILEO GALILEI
1564–1642
Italian natural philosopher, one of the first to take a modern scientific viewpoint

ROBERT HOOKE
1635–1703
Long-time opponent of Newton

30-SECOND TEXT
Brian Clegg

3-SECOND THRASH
Newton's second law tells us about the relationship between the force applied to a body and the change in its momentum or its acceleration.

3-MINUTE THOUGHT
In his dealings with Hooke Newton gained something of a reputation for not acknowledging those from whom he got ideas. But he was generous in the *Principia* in ascribing the first two laws to Galileo, saying that it was in using these that his Italian predecessor understood the falling of heavy bodies and the movement of projectiles. In reality, although there was some overlap, Galileo could not have conceived the second law as Newton did, as he did not have the concept of mass.

Galileo reputedly dropped a massive and a lighter object from the Leaning Tower of Pisa in Italy: both landed at the same time.

THE THIRD
LAW OF MOTION

the 30-second theory

RELATED TOPICS
See also
THE FIRST LAW OF MOTION
page 96

THE SECOND LAW OF MOTION
page 98

THE OCCULT ATTRACTION
page 122

3-SECOND THRASH
Newton's third law tells us that when one body acts on another, it experiences an equal and opposite reaction from the other body.

3-MINUTE THOUGHT
When Robert Goddard suggested in 1920 that a rocket could reach the Moon, the *New York Times* mocked him: 'That Professor Goddard … does not know the relation of action to reaction, and of the need to have something better than a vacuum against which to react – to say that would be absurd. Of course he only seems to lack the knowledge ladled out daily in high schools.' The newspaper missed that the action is on the exhaust gas and the reaction on the rocket.

The third of Newton's laws of motion is probably the most misunderstood. The commonly stated form 'Every action has an equal and opposite reaction' seems to imply that everything is happening to the same body, and that nothing can change as everything will be cancelled out. Newton's own formulation in *Principia* was rather different. He says, 'To any action there is always an opposite and equal reaction; in other words, the actions of two bodies on each other are always equal and in the opposite direction.' Newton goes on to give illustrations: 'If anyone presses on a stone with a finger, the finger is also pressed on by the stone. If a horse draws a stone tied to a rope, the horse will (so to speak) also be drawn equally towards the stone, for the rope stretched out at both ends, will urge the horse towards the stone and the stone towards the horse … and will impede the forward motion of the one as much as it promotes the forward motion of the other.' An essential understanding for constructing practically anything mechanical, this was the only one of Newton's 'axioms, or laws of motion' that he did not attribute to Galileo.

3-SECOND BIOGRAPHIES
GALILEO GALILEI
1564–1642
Italian natural philosopher who made detailed experimental studies of motion

ROBERT GODDARD
1882–1945
American engineer and rocket pioneer

30-SECOND TEXT
Brian Clegg

The rocket is thrust forwards and the exhaust gases, backwards; the cannonball, forward and the cannon itself, backwards.

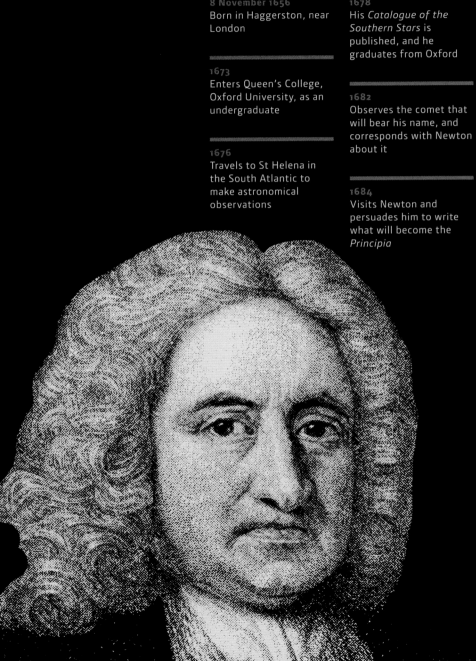

8 November 1656
Born in Haggerston, near London

1673
Enters Queen's College, Oxford University, as an undergraduate

1676
Travels to St Helena in the South Atlantic to make astronomical observations

1678
His *Catalogue of the Southern Stars* is published, and he graduates from Oxford

1682
Observes the comet that will bear his name, and corresponds with Newton about it

1684
Visits Newton and persuades him to write what will become the *Principia*

1686
Becomes Clerk of the Royal Society

1687
Newton's *Principia* is published at Halley's expense

1691
Invents a diving bell, and tests it himself

1698
Given command of the Navy ship *Paramore*, used for scientific research

1704
Becomes Savilian professor of geometry at Oxford University

1705
Publishes *A Synopsis of the Astronomy of Comets*

1710
Appointed Astronomer Royal at Greenwich Observatory

14 January 1742
Dies in Greenwich

EDMUND HALLEY

If it had not been for Edmund Halley, Newton's *Principia* might never have seen the light of day. It was Halley who persuaded Newton to write the book, and Halley who prepared it for publication at his own expense.

Halley was fascinated by astronomy from an early age. Before his 17th birthday he had started his studies at Oxford University, arriving there with a 7.3m (24ft)-long telescope superior to that of many professional astronomers. Three years later he hitched a ride on a ship bound for the island of St Helena, where he spent a year carrying out the first systematic observations of the night sky in the southern hemisphere. His *Catalogue of the Southern Stars* was published to great acclaim in November 1678; it was only the following month that the globetrotting student belatedly received his degree!

Halley's first contact with Newton came in 1682, when they corresponded about the comet of that year (a comet destined to play an important role in Halley's subsequent career). Two years later, eager to understand the physics underlying planetary orbits, Halley persuaded Newton to start writing the *Principia*. While Newton was working on it, Halley was appointed to the position of Clerk of the Royal Society, so it fell on him to see the book through to publication. This was something he was determined to do in spite of all adversity – even, as it turned out, having to pay for it out of his own pocket.

During his trip to St Helena Halley had become fascinated with the sea, and it became the focus of much of his research in the 1690s. He invented a diving bell that allowed him to work for up to two hours on the seabed, for example. Later he was given command of a Royal Navy ship, the *Paramore*, in which he made two long voyages to collect geomagnetic and meteorological data. It was only in the first decade of the 18th century that he finally settled down to a desk job – first as a professor at Oxford, and later as Astronomer Royal in Greenwich. During the first of these tenures Halley produced the work for which he is best known: *A Synopsis of the Astronomy of Comets*, in which he predicted that the comet of 1682 would return in 1758. It did, of course, although Halley never lived to see his prediction come true – he died in 1742.

Andrew May

INERTIA

the 30-second theory

In the world of everyday experience, things that are moving and that aren't being pushed stop. The Ancient Greeks assumed that this was the nature of reality. It was necessary to apply a force to keep something moving as it had a natural tendency to come to rest, either as close to the centre of the universe as it could if it had gravity, or as far away from the centre as it could if it had levity. But in our world we hardly ever see anything move without friction, the electromagnetic interaction between atoms slowing things down. Newton was able to see through the apparent reality to understand that moving bodies have inertia – a tendency to keep moving in the same straight line at the same speed unless something forces them to act differently. So, as he had with mass, Newton defined another new concept at the start of the *Principia*, which was inertia. He referred to this as the 'inherent force of matter' which 'is the power of resisting by which every body, so far as it is able, perseveres in its state either of resting or of moving uniformly straight forward'.

3-SECOND THRASH
Newton devised the concept of inertia, where a body at rest or in motion will keep doing the same thing unless a force acts on it to change things.

3-MINUTE THOUGHT
The term inertia was not new. Kepler had used it, but Newton was the first to apply it in its modern sense, changing its definition from a natural tendency to come to a stop to a natural tendency to continue in its current state unless something acted on it. He also uses *vis insita*, which is inherent or innate force, a term dating back to Horace, for the same concept.

RELATED TOPICS
See also
MASS VERSUS WEIGHT
page 94

THE FIRST LAW OF MOTION
page 96

CENTRIPETAL FORCE
page 106

3-SECOND BIOGRAPHIES
HORACE
65–68BC
Celebrated Roman lyric poet, properly known as Quintus Horatius Flaccus, who, like other classical poets, had an interest in natural philosophy

JOHANNES KEPLER
1571–1630
German astronomer and mathematician

30-SECOND TEXT
Brian Clegg

Inertia: A space shuttle would keep moving forever in a straight line unless a force acted on it.

CENTRIPETAL FORCE

the 30-second theory

Centripetal force was a concept that Newton introduced in the definitions at the start of *Principia*. He explained that centripetal force is a force like gravity or magnetism, where an object is drawn away from the straight line of its natural motion towards the centre of the object attracting it. Newton gave the useful example of a stone being whirled around in a sling. He pointed out that there had to be a force, channelled through the sling, that opposed the stone's 'endeavours' to leave the hand and drew the stone back towards the hand, so keeping it in orbit. This is one of the few cases where Newton admits to learning something from Robert Hooke. In a sequence of letters around the end of 1679, Hooke suggested to Newton that a body in orbit could be considered an effect of that body moving in a straight line while also accelerating towards the centre of the orbit. Newton replied that he had 'never heard of this hypothesis'. This seems to have inspired Newton's shift from considering the kind of centrifugal force espoused by Descartes to an inward-pointing centripetal force capable of producing Hooke's acceleration.

3-SECOND THRASH
Newton devised the concept of centripetal force that generates acceleration towards the centre of an attractive body to pull a moving object out of its natural straight-line motion.

3-MINUTE THOUGHT
Centripetal force seems counterintuitive because we assume that it takes a force to keep a body in motion. We think that when, for instance, an object shoots outwards when whirled around, there is an outward, 'centrifugal' force. In reality this is just the body attempting to continue in a straight line according to Newton's first law and takes no force. Instead, as Newton observed, if the object is pulled off course, it is because a centripetal force is making this happen.

RELATED TOPICS
See also
MASS VERSUS WEIGHT
page 94

THE FIRST LAW OF MOTION
page 96

THE ROTATING BUCKET
page 108

3-SECOND BIOGRAPHIES
RENÉ DESCARTES
1596–1650
French natural philosopher whose ideas on forces and light worked in opposition to those of Newton

ROBERT HOOKE
1635–1703
English natural philosopher and architect

30-SECOND TEXT
Brian Clegg

The Earth is both continuing in a straight line and accelerating in towards the Sun; the combined effect is its orbit.

THE ROTATING BUCKET

the 30-second theory

3-SECOND THRASH
Whether the water in a rotating bucket has a flat or curved surface depends on the absolute motion of the water, not its relative motion.

3-MINUTE THOUGHT
Persuasive as the bucket argument is from a scientific point of view, many philosophers have been uncomfortable with the concept of 'absolute space' that it implies. In 1883, the Austrian philosopher Ernst Mach suggested an alternative interpretation of the experiment in terms of *relative* motion of the water – not relative to the bucket, but to the entire cosmos. This idea, which remains controversial to this day, has become known as Mach's Principle.

Many of Newton's contemporaries, including Leibniz, believed that all motion was relative: if two objects had different motions, then either one of them could equally well be taken as being at rest. Newton disagreed: he believed this was only true for the case of uniform motion in a straight line. Non-uniform motion could only occur when there were external forces acting on a body, and this meant it had to be defined in *absolute* rather than relative terms. To illustrate the point, Newton described an experiment with a bucket of water suspended on a cord. When the bucket is stationary, there are no forces acting on the water and its surface remains flat. If the cord is then twisted many times and released, the bucket starts to spin round. At first, before the bucket's motion is communicated to the water, the surface of the latter remains flat – showing there are still no forces acting on it. As soon as the water starts to rotate, however, its edges rise up and the centre dips down. Yet its motion *relative to the bucket* is the same as it was when they were both stationary. Newton concluded that the curved surface could only be ascribed to motion in an absolute sense.

RELATED TOPICS
See also
THE FIRST LAW OF MOTION
page 96

INERTIA
page 104

CENTRIPETAL FORCE
page 106

3-SECOND BIOGRAPHIES
GOTTFRIED WILHELM LEIBNIZ
1646–1716
German philosopher who argued that physical phenomena are relative rather than absolute

ERNST MACH
1838–1916
Austrian physicist and philosopher who formulated Mach's Principle

30-SECOND TEXT
Andrew May

When both water and bucket are spinning, is there no relative motion? Newton thought so. Ernst Mach reconsidered.

GRAVITY

action at a distance Usually, to make something happen at a distance we expect something to travel from A to B, whether it's a rock to knock a tin off a fence or a sound wave in air to produce hearing. But Newton said that there was no such linkage in gravity: it was an action at a distance with nothing travelling from A to B.

Aristotle's theory of four elements
Although probably conceived by the earlier philosopher Empedocles, the idea that everything was made out of four elements was widely accepted due to the influence of the Ancient Greek philosopher Aristotle. The four elements were earth, air, fire and water. In this theory, earth and water had gravity, a tendency to head towards the centre of the universe, while the other two elements had the opposite, levity.

Boyle's law Also known as Mariotte's law, Boyle's law, named after Robert Boyle, states that the pressure of a gas is inversely proportional to its volume. As the volume increases, the pressure decreases and vice versa.

elliptical Having the shape of an ellipse – the shape produced by a loop of string rotated around two pins. The circle is a special case of the ellipse, where both pins are located at the same point. Because the Sun attracts a planet and the planet attracts the Sun, the result is an elliptical orbit, rather than a circular one. Kepler's laws of planetary motion assumed elliptical orbits.

inverse square law Technically any force that falls off with the square of the distance away from the source (for example, electromagnetism) is described as the inverse square law. But the law was most famously applied by Newton to the gravitational attraction between two bodies, which is proportional to the inverse of the squared distance between them.

Johannes Kepler Kepler was a contemporary of Galileo whose laws of planetary motion were derived from observation. Newton was able to provide a mathematical basis for Kepler's laws derived from Newton's law of universal gravitation.

levity Once the opposite of gravity, levity was the tendency for light elements to head away from the centre of the universe, although it has now largely come to mean something light in the sense of not being serious.

occult In the way it was used here, occult means hidden, not accessible to the senses.

parabola A symmetrical curve like an opened-out U that is approximately the trajectory of a comet around the Sun and is the typical path of a projectile, combining steady forward motion with an acceleration at right angles.

Principia Newton's masterpiece, *Philosophiæ Naturalis Principia Mathematica* ('Mathematical Principles of Natural Philosophy') as it is more properly known, gave us his three laws of motion and his law of universal gravitation, showing that the same principle is responsible for an apple falling and for planets orbiting the Sun. The book was published in 1687 in Latin and was deliberately made less than easy to read, as Newton wanted to limit its audience to experienced natural philosophers.

pure attractive force Explanations of gravity in Newton's time either assumed that a material (the ether) filled space, and that movement in this material produced a kind of suction, or that a body shielded another body from a repulsive force, and by reducing repulsion caused a force in the opposite direction. Newton disposed of these hypotheses and simply represented gravity as an attraction between two bodies requiring no intermediaries. Such an 'action at a distance' was considered 'occult'.

vortices Plural of vortex, vortices were central to Descartes' model for gravity. He assumed all space was filled with an invisible substance and that a massive object distorted this ether causing attractive 'whirlpools' that pulled bodies towards each other.

FROM TENDENCY TO ATTRACTION

the 30-second theory

RELATED TOPICS
See also
MASS VERSUS WEIGHT
page 94

THE OCCULT ATTRACTION
page 122

THE INVERSE SQUARE LAW
page 128

3-SECOND THRASH
Newton did not just mathematically describe gravity, he changed its philosophical nature from a tendency towards the centre of the universe to an attraction between bodies.

3-MINUTE THOUGHT
The classical view of gravity was why Aristotle's (incorrect) idea that heavy objects fell faster than lighter ones seemed plausible. Heavy objects had more stuff in them that wanted to get to the centre of the universe. This model of gravity was one of the reasons that medieval science found it difficult to move the Earth away from the centre of the universe. To do so also undermined the accepted mechanisms of nature.

It is easy to concentrate on the mathematics behind Newton's work on gravity, but just as revolutionary was his transformation of our understanding of the *nature* of gravity. Ever since the Ancient Greeks, gravity had been seen as one half of a pair of tendencies. Two elements – earth and water – had gravity, while the other two – air and fire – had levity. Gravity made heavy elements seek out the centre of the universe, which in Greek cosmology was the centre of the Earth. Light elements wanted to get away from the centre. This was a result of an inherent tendency that was part of the nature of heavy things. Gravity made heavy things tend towards the centre of the universe, just as dogs tended to attack cats. As the 12th-century natural philosopher Adelard of Bath said, 'What is heavy stays best in the lowest position. Every thing loves that which preserves its life. But it tends towards that which it loves. Therefore it is necessary that every earthy thing tends towards the lowest of all positions.' Newton took away the special nature of a particular point in the universe and transformed gravity into the attraction between any two bodies with mass.

3-SECOND BIOGRAPHIES
ARISTOTLE
384–322BC
Ancient Greek philosopher

ADELARD OF BATH
c.1080–c.1152
English natural philosopher, translated ancient Greek and Arab science works into Latin

30-SECOND TEXT
Brian Clegg

The Ancient Greek view: earth and water have gravity (tend towards the universe's centre); air and fire have levity (tend away from the centre).

NEWTON AND THE APPLE

the 30-second theory

Many think that the story of Newton and the apple is simply a myth. One aspect certainly is. No one, other than cartoonists, has ever suggested that Newton was inspired by an apple falling on his head. But the main apple story did come from Newton's lips. Antiquarian William Stukeley described a visit he paid to Newton on 15 April 1726, at Newton's lodgings in Orbell's Buildings in Kensington Church Street (now in London, but then still in the country). Stukeley related: 'After dinner, the weather being warm, we went into the garden, and drank thea under the shade of some apple trees; only he and myself. Amidst other discourse, he told me, he was just in the same situation, as when formerly, the notion of gravitation came into his mind. Why should that apple always descend perpendicularly to the ground, thought he to himself; occasion'd by the fall of an apple, as he sat in a contemplative mood. Why should it not go sideways, or upwards? But constantly to the earths centre? Assuredly the reason is, that the earth draws it. There must be a drawing power in matter … If matter thus draws matter; it must be in proportion of its quantity. Therefore the apple draws the earth, as well as the earth draws the apple.'

RELATED TOPICS
See also
FROM TENDENCY TO ATTRACTION
page 114

THE INVERSE SQUARE LAW
page 128

GRAVITATIONAL MUSINGS
page 130

3-SECOND BIOGRAPHIES
HANNAH AYSCOUGH (NEWTON)
1623–79
Newton's mother, owner of Woolsthorpe Manor and the apple tree

WILLIAM STUKELEY
1687–1765
English antiquarian who wrote *Memoirs of Sir Isaac Newton's Life*

30-SECOND TEXT
Brian Clegg

3-SECOND THRASH
Thinking about an apple at his home in Woolsthorpe may have given Newton the inspiration to think more about gravity (but it didn't fall on his head).

3-MINUTE THOUGHT
Stukeley also tells us: 'Thus by degrees, he began to apply this property of gravitation to the motion of the earth, and of the heavenly bodys: to consider their distances, their magnitudes, their periodical revolutions: to find out, that this property, conjointly with a progressive motion impressed on them in the beginning, perfectly solv'd their circular courses; kept the planets from falling upon one another, or dropping all together into one center,' expanding the idea to planetary motion.

The apple tree that inspired Newton is still standing at Woolsthorpe Manor.

ORBITS

the 30-second theory

We have a big advantage over Newton and his contemporaries. We have seen what happens when objects in space obey the first law of motion. Rockets show the effectiveness of the third law. And dropping a hammer and a feather on the Moon directly shows that objects with different mass fall at the same rate if there is no air to get in the way. Similarly, astronauts on the International Space Station demonstrate an essential aspect of being in orbit. On the space station, people float around. Not because the Earth's gravity is weak there – it's about 90 per cent of the surface value – but because they are in free fall, accelerating towards the Earth. The people and the station fall at the same rate, so the people float. As Newton realized with the assistance of Robert Hooke, the reason that objects in orbit are falling but don't crash into the ground is because they are also in motion at right angles to the surface, and the two motions – sideways and downwards – cancel each other out. Newton was able to portray being in orbit as falling, but forever missing.

RELATED TOPICS
See also
CENTRIPETAL FORCE
page 106

PLANETARY MOTION
page 136

COMETS
page 150

3-SECOND BIOGRAPHIES
GALILEO GALILEI
1564–1642
Italian natural philosopher who explained the trajectory of projectiles

ROBERT HOOKE
1635–1703
English natural philosopher who spotted the nature of an orbit

30-SECOND TEXT
Brian Clegg

3-SECOND THRASH
An object in orbit is in free fall towards the body it orbits, but it is also moving at right angles to the body, and at just the right speed to keep missing.

3-MINUTE THOUGHT
Newton already knew that a curved path in the form of a parabola could be generated from the combination of two types of motion, one at a steady rate forwards in a straight line and the other an acceleration downwards, because this appears in Galileo's analysis of the motion of projectiles. But it seems that he had not applied this thinking to circular and elliptical orbits until Hooke's observation caused him to look at things differently.

An orbiting object – or scientist on a space station – is accelerating towards the Earth in free fall, but also travels forward, continuously missing.

HYPOTHESES NON FINGO

the 30-second theory

When Newton produced the second edition of the *Principia* in 1713, he added a 'General Scholium' to clarify a number of points that he felt critics of the first edition had misunderstood. One thing he wanted to emphasize in particular was that everything in the book was rigorously derived from observed phenomena. Where he had not been able to do that, he had simply remained silent. For example, while he had been able to *describe* the force of gravity, he could not say what the ultimate source of it was. Some readers had seen this as a weakness of the book, but Newton maintained that was not the case. Such interpretations were necessarily going to be speculative; hence they had no place in a rigorous work of science. He referred to such speculations as 'hypotheses', and expressed his disdain for them in the famous Latin phrase *hypotheses non fingo*. This has been translated in a number of ways, but the gist of it is: 'I do not invent hypotheses.' He goes on to say: 'For whatever is not deduced from the phenomena is to be called an hypothesis; and hypotheses, whether metaphysical or physical, whether of occult qualities or mechanical, have no place in experimental philosophy.'

3-SECOND THRASH
In his published work, Newton carefully avoided inventing speculative hypotheses to explain his law of gravity; he believed the law itself should be enough.

3-MINUTE THOUGHT
In his earliest scientific writings, Newton was not so careful to avoid mingling hard facts and 'hypotheses' as he became later on. While his great discoveries in optics, such as the splitting of white light into colours, were firmly based on observation, his attempt to explain these discoveries in the context of a particle theory was a different matter: he even called one of his early papers 'An Hypothesis Explaining the Properties of Light'.

RELATED TOPICS
See also
PARTICLES OF LIGHT
page 26

THE OCCULT ATTRACTION
page 122

GRAVITATIONAL MUSINGS
page 130

3-SECOND BIOGRAPHIES
ROBERT HOOKE
1635–1703
Opponent of Newton who dismissed his optics work as founded on 'hypotheses'

GOTTFRIED WILHELM LEIBNIZ
1646–1716
Prominent critic of the *Principia*, whose arguments Newton countered in the "General Scholium"

30-SECOND TEXT
Andrew May

Newton set out to describe how gravity works, not to speculate about where it comes from. Hypotheses were not for him, he said.

THE OCCULT ATTRACTION

the 30-second theory

RELATED TOPICS
See also
FROM TENDENCY TO
ATTRACTION
page 114

NEWTON AND THE APPLE
page 116

HYPOTHESES NON FINGO
page 120

GRAVITATIONAL MUSINGS
page 130

3-SECOND THRASH
Newton tried to protect his approach that used an attraction acting at a distance by limiting it to mathematics rather than physics, but his critics attacked it anyway.

3-MINUTE THOUGHT
The word 'attraction' did not help. At the time this was not used for the action of gravity or magnetism, really only applying in the sense of an 'attractive' person. Huygens' criticism of the approach being 'occult' did not refer to magic, but rather that the mechanism was hidden and unknown, lacking a simple physical cause for the force. Newton tried to take the line that it didn't matter as long as the maths worked – but others did not agree.

In some parts of the *Principia*, Newton emphasizes that he is merely working on a mathematical system, rather than on the realities of nature – he explicitly says that he is concerned with mathematics and 'putting aside any debates concerning physics'. The reason for this is that he was rightly concerned that the concept of 'attraction' between bodies with mass would cause trouble with his critics. Most natural philosophers of the day, taking the lead from René Descartes, abhorred the idea of an attraction that could act at a distance without anything intervening. They assumed that apparently empty space was filled with something that could transfer a force to produce the effect of gravity. But Newton's mathematics described a pure attractive force. His attempts to pretend that this was just a mathematical oddity failed. Huygens remarked 'I have nothing against him not being a Cartesian, provided he does not give us suppositions like that of attraction.' He wrote later that 'Attraction is not explainable by any of the principles of Mechanics, or of the rules of motion' and proclaimed that Newton's approach to gravity was 'in effect, to return to occult qualities and, even worse, to inexplicable ones'.

3-SECOND BIOGRAPHIES
RENÉ DESCARTES
1596–1650
French philosopher who believed that space was filled with an 'ether'

CHRISTIAAN HUYGENS
1629–95
Dutch natural philosopher who championed the wave theory of light

30-SECOND TEXT
Brian Clegg

Newton dismissed the idea of the ether. His theory of gravity caused upset because it posited an invisible attraction between objects.

TIDES

the 30-second theory

Twice-daily ocean tides are among the few phenomena on the Earth's surface that display the predictable regularity usually associated with celestial bodies. This led to the suggestion, made by Kepler and others, that tides were somehow caused by the attraction of the Moon. Without an obvious mechanism for the attraction, however, this notion smacked of the occult, and Kepler's contemporary Galileo rejected it in favour of an alternative – and ultimately incorrect – explanation. It was left to Newton, using his new theory of gravity, to show that tides are indeed caused by the Moon. Due to the inverse square law, the oceans on the side of the Earth closest to the Moon feel a stronger force than the planet as a whole, and so bulge upwards. At the same time, the oceans on the opposite side feel a weaker force, and so they too bulge away from the surface. Newton also realized that tides are affected by the Sun as well as the Moon. The Sun exerts a much stronger gravitational pull than the Moon, but it varies less from one side of the planet to the other because the Sun is so much further away. The net result is that the tidal effect of the Sun is about half that of the Moon.

RELATED TOPICS
See also
THE INVERSE SQUARE LAW
page 128

THE THREE-BODY PROBLEM
page 140

3-SECOND BIOGRAPHIES
JOHANNES KEPLER
1571–1630
German astronomer who speculated that tides were caused by the Moon

GALILEO GALILEI
1564–1642
Pioneering Italian scientist who rejected the idea that the Moon causes tides

30-SECOND TEXT
Andrew May

3-SECOND THRASH
The Earth's tides are caused by the difference in strength of the Moon's – and to a lesser extent the Sun's – gravity on opposite sides of the planet.

3-MINUTE THOUGHT
Actual tides are affected by several factors, also including the rotation of the Earth-Moon system, ocean dynamics and the distribution of land masses. As well as the familiar daily cycle, there is a slower cycle of spring tides, which have the largest tidal range, and neap tides with the smallest. Newton showed that spring tides occur when the Moon and Sun line up to act together, while neap tides occur when the two bodies work against each other.

Both Sun and Moon control the tides, the Moon significantly more. Effects of gravity makes the seawaters bulge.

25 January 1627
Born in Lismore, County Waterford, Ireland

1635
Attends Eton College

1638
Removed from Eton and begins home tuition

1639
Begins first European tour

1642
Arrives in Florence around the time Galileo dies in nearby Arcetri

1644
Returns to England and stays with his sister Katherine

1646
Becomes involved with the Invisible College

1652
Returns to Ireland

1654
Moves to Oxford

1661
Writes *The Sceptical Chemist*

1662
Writes an appendix to his 1660 *New Experiments Physio-Mechanicall, Touching the Spring of the Air and its Effects* which includes a form of 'Boyle's law'

1668
Moves to London

1680
Turns down position of President of the Royal Society because he is not prepared to swear an oath

31 December 1691
Dies in London

ROBERT BOYLE

There is good evidence that a major influence on Newton's early thinking was reading the work of Robert Boyle. Boyle's father, Richard, was earl of Cork and one of the richest men in Britain. Although Robert, as seventh son, did not inherit a title, he had a family with enough money to support him and enable him to pursue his interests.

Educated at Eton and then by a private tutor, Boyle spent a considerable time in his teens touring Europe, arriving in Italy around the time of Galileo's death, which is said to have influenced Boyle's studies in the future. The English Civil War and its precursors made things difficult for Boyle, whose father had died, leaving him primarily funded by other family members. In this period, Boyle was one of the founder members of the 'Invisible College' that fed into the Royal Society of London, giving him a chance to explore his scientific thinking further.

With the triumph of Oliver Cromwell in the civil war, Boyle – who had managed to stay largely neutral – was awarded sufficient lands in Ireland to have no further financial pressures for the rest of his life. At the invitation of John Wilkins, a leading light in the Invisible College, and finding it difficult to get scientific equipment in Ireland, Boyle moved to Oxford, joining the likes of John Wallis and Christopher Wren. It was there that he published his most important work. This included *The Sceptical Chemist*, which arguably marks the first big step in the move from alchemy to chemistry, dismissing Aristotle's theory of four elements.

Boyle had also been working on gases, using an air pump devised by Robert Hooke: he showed that sound could not travel through a vacuum and established the relationship between volume and pressure in a gas that would become known as Boyle's law. (Boyle was, in fact, beaten to this finding by another early Royal Society fellow, Henry Power, but it was Boyle's name that stuck. To add to the confusion, it is sometimes referred to as Mariotte's law, though the French physicist Edme Mariotte would not discover it for another 14 years.) Another significant aspect of Boyle's influence on Newton was his insistence on the importance of mathematics in all branches of science, pointing the way to Newton's mechanical universe. In 1668 Boyle moved to London, where he remained and continued to work in science for the rest of his life.

Brian Clegg

THE INVERSE SQUARE LAW

the 30-second theory

At the heart of Newton's work

was the idea that gravitation is an inverse square law. The modern statement of Newton's gravitational equation is that the attractive force is equal to Gm_1m_2/r^2 – in other words, it is equal to the gravitational constant, G (not to be confused with g, which is the acceleration at sea level due to the Earth's gravity), multiplied by the mass of each of the two bodies and divided by the square of the distance between the bodies. This equation does not appear in the *Principia*, though it is implied. The key aspect that the force varies with the inverse square of the distance had been theorized for a number of years before the publication of the *Principia*. Notably, Robert Hooke had made the observation, and accused Newton of plagiarism for stealing his idea. Hooke had certainly written in 1666 that the force of gravity increased as an object got closer to the attracting body and later wrote to Newton that there was a supposition that it was an inverse square effect. However, unlike Newton, he was never able to demonstrate this mathematically, and Newton was able to show that he had discussed the inverse square hypothesis with Christopher Wren before Hooke's letters were sent.

RELATED TOPICS
See also
FROM TENDENCY TO ATTRACTION
page 114

GRAVITATIONAL MUSINGS
page 130

3-SECOND BIOGRAPHIES
ROBERT HOOKE
1635–1703
British natural philosopher, was long-term opponent of Newton

CHRISTOPHER WREN
1632–1723
British architect and founder member of the Royal Society

HENRY CAVENDISH
1731–1810
British natural philosopher

30-SECOND TEXT
Brian Clegg

Cavendish, whose work produced a value for the gravitational constant, also devised experiments to investigate the properties of air, electrical attraction and the weight of the Earth.

3-SECOND THRASH
Newton demonstrated that gravitational attraction would be proportional to the masses of the bodies involved and inversely proportional to the square of the distance between them.

3-MINUTE THOUGHT
The gravitational constant, G, which makes it possible to produce absolute values for the attractive force of gravity, was not in *Principia*, which only deals with values that are proportional to each other. The constant was first deduced from measurements made by Henry Cavendish in 1798, well after Newton's death, and has proved difficult to measure accurately, because gravity is a very weak force, so the attraction between two weights in a measuring apparatus is very small.

GRAVITATIONAL MUSINGS

the 30-second theory

Newton was careful to suggest that he was presenting a mathematical approach that matched observation and would not guess as to how gravity worked at a distance. Yet he did have a theory. His main concern was to keep hypothetical solutions separate from thorough mathematical expositions. He explicitly dismissed Descartes' idea that planetary motion was caused by vortices in the ether. However, in various places Newton suggested that there might be a similarity between the cause of gravity and a 'subtle spirit'. This is not a ghostly phenomenon, but rather 'a subtle spirit or Agent latent in bodies by which Electrical Attraction and many other phaenomena may be performed'. He refers in an early draft of the closing part of the *Principia* to electrical experiments at the Royal Society by Francis Hauksbee that demonstrated attraction on a small scale. Newton did not think that gravity was the *same* as electrical or magnetic attraction, noting that 'the laws of these are very different from the laws of gravity', but nevertheless felt that there was a familial relationship and that discovering more about these different types of attraction would eventually provide an explanation for the attractive force of gravity.

RELATED TOPICS
See also
FROM TENDENCY TO
ATTRACTION
page 114

NEWTON AND THE APPLE
page 116

HYPOTHESES NON FINGO
page 120

3-SECOND BIOGRAPHIES
FRANCIS HAUKSBEE
1660–1713
British natural philosopher who worked on static electricity

NICOLAS FATIO DE DUILLIER
1654–1753
Swiss mathematician who proposed a mechanical mechanism to explain gravity

GEORGES-LOUIS LE SAGE
1724–1803
Swiss natural philosopher who expanded de Duiller's mechanical theory

30-SECOND TEXT
Brian Clegg

Georges-Louise le Sage also contributed to the Encyclopédie of Diderot and d'Alembert.

3-SECOND THRASH
Newton might have claimed that he framed no hypotheses, but he did have an idea that gravity had a similar cause to electrical and magnetic attraction.

3-MINUTE THOUGHT
In later years a mechanical explanation for gravity emerged of which Newton would probably have approved. Proposed by de Duillier and Le Sage, and later updated by Lord Kelvin, this theory proposed that there was a constant stream of particles crossing the universe in all directions. The push these gave to bodies cancelled out. But if something screened the particles from one direction, a body would feel a pull towards that screening body – an attraction.

BEYOND EARTH

equinox The Earth's rotational axis (a line through the north and south poles) is on a slant as it moves round the Sun. This means that in its orbit there are two points in the year when the axis is at 90 degrees to a line between the Earth and the Sun – these are the equinoxes.

Flamsteed's star catalogue Newton needed astronomical data to update the *Principia*, which he obtained from Astronomer Royal John Flamsteed by asking his royal connections to commission a catalogue of the skies.

Gauss's law Derived in the 19th century by Carl Friedrich Gauss to describe the way electric charges produce an electric field, Gauss's law is a sophisticated mathematical approach to an inverse square law that can be applied to gravitation.

inverse square law gravitation Any force that falls off with the square of the distance away from the source (for example, electromagnetism) is described by the inverse square law. However, the law was most famously applied by Newton to gravitational attraction.

Kepler's law of planetary motion Johannes Kepler was a contemporary of Galileo whose laws of planetary motion were derived from observation. Kepler's laws were that: the orbit of a planet is an ellipse with the Sun at one focus; a line linking a planet to the Sun will sweep out equal areas in equal times; and that the square of the time taken to complete an orbit is proportional to the cube of the distance between the centre of the ellipse of the orbit and the orbit's most distant point.

Keplerian ellipse Johannes Kepler deduced from observational data that planets travel in an ellipse around the Sun, with the Sun at one of the two 'foci' of the ellipse (an ellipse's equivalent of the centre of a circle). This is a Keplerian ellipse.

Newton's theory of gravity While Newton was enthusiastic to insist that he 'framed no hypothesis' as to how gravity worked, he did have a theory, based on the impact of a stream of particles flowing through the universe.

parabola A symmetrical curve like an opened-out U that is approximately the trajectory of a comet around the Sun and is the typical path of a projectile, combining steady forward motion with an acceleration at right angles.

perturbation A modification of a planet's orbit from that predicted by the masses of the planet and its star, caused by the gravitational attraction of other bodies.

precession A rotating body, like the Earth, spins around an axis of rotation (in the case of the Earth, a line through the north and south poles). If the direction of that axis itself rotates with time, that extra rotation is called a precession. This happens with the Earth, which causes the timing of the equinoxes to shift, producing the 'precession of the equinoxes'.

shell theorem To produce his law of gravity, Newton had to work out how all the different parts of an object add up to produce a force. He proved that it was possible to treat a body like the Earth as if all its mass were concentrated at a point in its centre, and also that for a hollow spherical shell, however massive, there will be no gravitational force with that shell.

three-body problem Newton's law of universal gravitation makes it possible to work out exactly what the force will be between two bodies, like the Earth and the Sun. However, add in one more body and it becomes impossible to produce a complete solution to the way they will act. We can approximate very closely to an answer, but it will always be an approximation. This is the three-body problem.

two-body problem Newton's law of gravity precisely defines the interaction of two massive bodies, like the Earth and the Sun (or an apple and the Earth). This is the two-body problem, in contrast to the three-body problem.

PLANETARY MOTION

the 30-second theory

3-SECOND THRASH
The structure of the Ancient Greek universe had already been disproved, but Newton went further in applying the same universal gravitation to the planets as to an apple.

3-MINUTE THOUGHT
Newton goes about this in an odd way. He says that he originally wrote the third book in a 'popular form', but rewrote it to restrict the readership to those who understood the mathematics. Strangely, rather than start from the elliptical orbits expected from Kepler's work, Newton first assumes circular orbits and demonstrates why the planets should obey an inverse square law, then deduces from the mathematics that the orbits actually have to be elliptical.

Since the Ancient Greeks there had been an assumption that what happened within the orbit of the Moon (the sublunar realm) was entirely different to the rest of the universe. There was even a separate element, the quintessence, to make up the perfection of the environment that began with the Moon of untarnished circles and spheres. This picture had been shaken by the Copernican universe and shattered by Kepler's laws of planetary motion, which put the paths of planets on ellipses, rather than 'perfect' circles. Yet despite this, most natural philosophers of Newton's time still had the vestiges of the Greek system setting their world-view. Specifically, the assumption was that the mechanism that kept the planets in their orbits and the workings of gravity on Earth were entirely separate. But Newton conceived of a universal law of gravity, one that would explain the path of the Earth around the Sun as well as it did the fall of an apple to the Earth. He set out in the third book of the *Principia*, entitled 'The System of the World', to explain the way that the planets and their moons move, governed by his inverse square law gravitation.

RELATED TOPICS
See also
ORBITS
page 118

THE INVERSE SQUARE LAW
page 128

THE THREE-BODY PROBLEM
page 140

3-SECOND BIOGRAPHIES
NICOLAUS COPERNICUS
1473–1543
Polish deviser of the heliocentric model of the universe

JOHANNES KEPLER
1571–1630
German astronomer who derived laws of planetary motion

30-SECOND TEXT
Brian Clegg

Johannes Kepler announced the first two of his three laws of planetary motion – establishing that the planets move in elliptical orbits around the Sun – in 1609.

WHERE IS A BODY?

the 30-second theory

When Newton watched the apple fall, the thing that puzzled him most was why the apple should drop vertically downwards, as if it were being pulled towards the exact centre of the Earth. According to his theory of a universal force of gravity, every tiny piece of matter should attract every other tiny piece. That meant the apple was subjected to innumerable forces coming from all the different parts of the planet. Why should the net force be precisely towards the centre? His eventual solution of the problem, which appeared in the *Principia*, is known as the shell theorem. This describes the gravitational force exerted on an object by a thin spherical shell of material. If the object is outside the shell, it feels the same force as it would if all the mass of the shell were concentrated at its centre. Since the Earth can be thought of as a large number of concentric shells, this explains why the force on any object on its surface – or in orbit around it – is directed exactly towards its centre. Newton's geometrical proof of the shell theorem was quite convoluted, but it is mathematically easier to prove using a more modern method called a surface integral, which combines the gravitational fields in a variant of Gauss's law, usually applied to electricity.

RELATED TOPICS
See also
NEWTON AND THE APPLE
page 116

THE INVERSE SQUARE LAW
page 128

3-SECOND BIOGRAPHY
CARL FRIEDRICH GAUSS
1777–1855
German mathematician who produced an alternative formulation of Newton's law of gravity

30-SECOND TEXT
Andrew May

3-SECOND THRASH
The gravitational force due to a spherical body like the Earth is the same as if all the mass of the body was concentrated at its centre.

3-MINUTE THOUGHT
The shell theorem also predicts the gravitational force on an object *inside* the shell: in this case the force is exactly zero. This means that if one were to dig vertically downwards towards the centre of the planet, one would only feel the gravity of material lower down, not higher up. At the very centre of the Earth, the force of gravity would drop to zero.

Thinking of Earth as a series of shells and using the shell theorem, Newton explained why anywhere on the planet we feel gravity pulling towards the Earth's centre.

THE THREE-BODY PROBLEM

the 30-second theory

3-SECOND THRASH

Newton obtained approximate solutions to the gravitational problem of three bodies – such as the Sun, Earth and Moon – but it cannot be solved exactly.

3-MINUTE THOUGHT

Although there is no general mathematical solution to the three-body problem, it can be tackled in specific cases by solving Newton's equations on a digital computer. One of the first people to do this was Michael Minovitch, who applied the theory to the case of spacecraft trajectories in the 1960s. He discovered the 'gravitational slingshot' technique, whereby a spacecraft moving through the solar system can boost its speed each time it passes close to a planet.

The simplest application of Newton's theory of gravity is to the problem of two bodies, for example a planet orbiting the Sun or a satellite orbiting the Earth. In this case the equations have an exact solution, corresponding in effect to Kepler's laws of planetary motion. It is rarely the case, however, that two bodies can be taken in complete isolation from other gravitational influences. The three-body problem is the next step up in complexity, and while it is a small step in numerical terms it is an enormous one in mathematical complexity. The classic three-body problem is that of the Earth, Moon and Sun: Newton grappled with this for years with only partial success. The orbit of the Moon around the Earth can be predicted fairly accurately if it is approximated as a Keplerian ellipse subject to the perturbing effect of the Sun's gravity. However, there is no general solution of the three-body problem in the same way there is for the two-body problem. This is not just a limitation of human ingenuity, but an inherent feature of the mathematics – a fact that was proven by the French mathematician Henri Poincaré at the end of the 19th century.

RELATED TOPICS

See also
PLANETARY MOTION
page 136

MOTION OF THE MOON
page 142

PERTURBATION
page 144

3-SECOND BIOGRAPHIES

JOHANNES KEPLER
1571–1630
German astronomer who outlined three laws of planetary motion

HENRI POINCARÉ
1854–1912
French mathematician who analysed the three-body problem

MICHAEL MINOVITCH
1936–
American who applied the three-body problem to spacecraft trajectories

30-SECOND TEXT
Andrew May

A spacecraft can bump up its speed using the gravitational attraction of planets it passes.

MOTION OF THE MOON

the 30-second theory

Newton used the Moon to check
the effectiveness of universal gravitation, in
'the Moon test.' He began by establishing the
distance between the Earth and the Moon from
various astronomers' measurements (correcting
an error by Tycho) as 'roughly 60 terrestrial
semidiameters'. This isn't a bad estimate: the
real orbit varies between 56.9 and 63.6 times
the Earth's radius, averaging 60.3. Next, he
imagined that the Moon stopped in its orbit and
fell under the force of gravity. He calculated,
using his inverse square law, that the Moon
would fall '15 Paris feet, 1 inch and 1 4/9 lines' in
a minute, where a line is one-twelfth of an inch.
He worked out what the equivalent would be for
the Moon at the Earth's surface and found it to
be the same as experienced by 'a Pendulum
beating seconds in the latitude of Paris ... as
Huygens observed.' Triumphantly he noted:
'And therefore that force by which the moon is
kept in its orbit, in descending from the moon's
orbit to the surface of the earth, comes out
equal to the force of gravity here on earth, and
so (by rules 1 and 2) is that very force that we
call gravity.'

RELATED TOPICS
See also
ORBITS
page 118

THE INVERSE SQUARE LAW
page 126

PLANETARY MOTION
page 136

3-SECOND BIOGRAPHIES
TYCHO BRAHE
1546–1601
Danish astronomer who erred
in calculating the distance to
the Moon

CHRISTIAAN HUYGENS
1629–95
Dutch natural philosopher

30-SECOND TEXT
Brian Clegg

3-SECOND THRASH
Newton used known
facts about the Moon to
see how it would fall if it
were not in motion, and
from this established the
universal nature of gravity.

3-MINUTE THOUGHT
Rules 1 and 2 come at the
start of the book, stating
that 'No more causes of
natural things should be
admitted than are both
true and sufficient to
explain their phenomena'
and 'Therefore the causes
assigned to natural effects
of the same kind must be,
so far as possible, the
same.' This is similar to the
approach that Einstein
took in producing his
principle of equivalence,
which equated acceleration
and gravitation.

*Newton performed
his celebrated Moon
Test thought
experiment in 1684 and
included it in the first
edition of the Principia.*

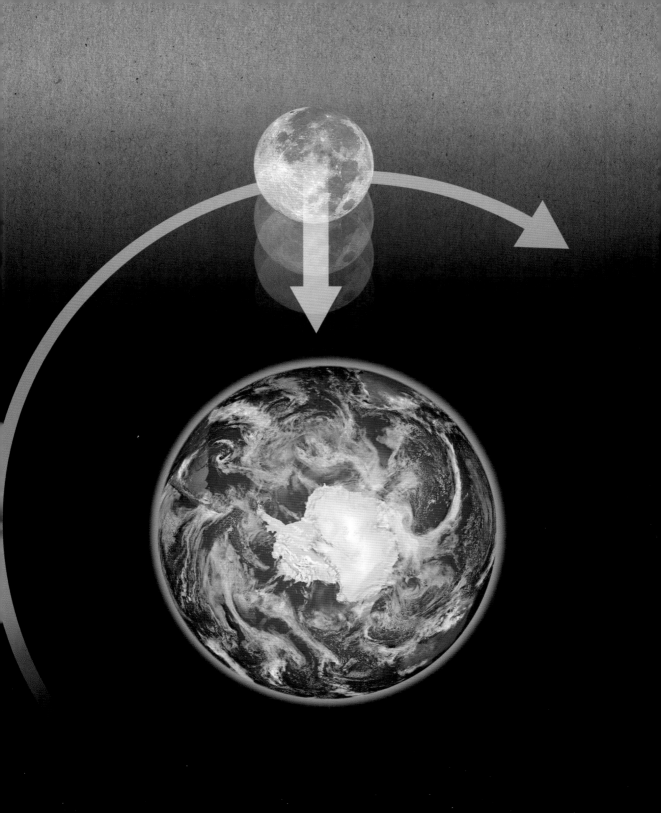

PERTURBATION

the 30-second theory

It's easy to imagine now, when we have equipment like the Hubble Space Telescope, that astronomy in Newton's day, less than a century after Galileo discovered the first four moons of Jupiter, was extremely limited. And yet one of Newton's key arguments for his universal gravitation – showing that his mathematics did not just work for bodies that were relatively near the Earth – concerned the influence that Jupiter had on the orbit of Saturn. Both these planets are visible with the naked eye, and so had been known since ancient times, but Newton was making a subtle observation, realizing that giants like Jupiter and Saturn would have a significant gravitational influence on anything in their neighbourhoods. As Newton put it in the *Principia*: 'Jupiter and Saturn near conjunction, by attracting each other, sensibly perturb each other's motion.' In practice, while Newton was right conceptually, his attempts to predict values for the perturbation were inevitably flawed because he was dealing, effectively, with a three-body problem with the Sun, Jupiter and Saturn all having significant influence, resulting in an outcome that can't be fully solved without some limitation or approximation. This wasn't helped by the actual perturbations being sufficiently small to be almost undetectable by the telescopes of Newton's day.

RELATED TOPICS
See also
THE INVERSE SQUARE LAW
page 128

PLANETARY MOTION
page 136

THE THREE-BODY PROBLEM
page 140

3-SECOND BIOGRAPHIES
GALILEO GALILEI
1564–1642
Italian natural philosopher who discovered four moons of Jupiter

JOHANNES KEPLER
1571–1630
German astronomer and mathematician

JOHN FLAMSTEED
1646–1719
English astronomer who was the first Astronomer Royal

30-SECOND TEXT
Brian Clegg

Flamsteed confirmed that there were perturbations in the solar orbits of Jupiter and Saturn – proof of the effects of gravity.

3-SECOND THRASH
Newton predicted correctly that planets like Jupiter and Saturn, when their orbits came close, would have sufficient influence on each other to shift the direction of the orbits.

3-MINUTE THOUGHT
Newton asked Astronomer Royal John Flamsteed if he had observed unexpected variations in the motion of Saturn, compared with Kepler's orbital predictions. Flamsteed agreed that there were, but considered them small enough to be observational errors. He concluded 'I can scarce thinke there should be any such influence ... in such yielding matter as our aether, I cannot conceave that any impression made by the one planet upon it can disturbe the motion of the other.'

PRECESSION

the 30-second theory

By Newton's day, it had been known for 1,800 years that the Earth's axis went through a slow rotation, producing the precession of the equinoxes. But a real triumph of Newton's new mathematics of gravitation was to suggest the correct reason for this. It was known that the Earth is not a perfect sphere, since it has a bulge around the equator (due to the Earth's rotation). Newton realized that because of the tilt of the Earth's axis, both the Sun and the Moon would have a pull that was greater on the nearer part of the bulge, and less on the more distant part. This, he calculated, would have an influence on the direction of the Earth's axis that would cause it to rotate slowly, sweeping out a cone shape – an effect that he calculated should produce pretty much exactly the precession that was observed. He does this in an ingenious manner, going from the perturbation of a moon to a continuous ring of moons, which becomes the equatorial bulge. As several times in Newton's key work, the assumptions he used were not entirely correct, so his calculation of values that were very close to those observed was suspicious, yet his explanation has been confirmed correct.

RELATED TOPICS
See also
INVENTING DATA
page 28

THE INVERSE SQUARE LAW
page 128

PERTURBATION
page 144

3-SECOND BIOGRAPHIES
HIPPARCHUS
C.190–120BC
Ancient Greek astronomer who discovered the precession of the equinoxes

CLAUDIUS PTOLEMY
c.85–165
Greco-Roman astronomer whose work formed the basis of astronomical theory through to Newton

30-SECOND TEXT
Brian Clegg

3-SECOND THRASH
Newton used his gravitational theory to explain the precession of the equinoxes as the influence of the Sun and the Moon on the Earth's equatorial bulge.

3-MINUTE THOUGHT
The equinoxes in spring and autumn – which split the two half-years between summer and winter solstices – are the points in the Earth's orbit when our planet's axis is not tilted towards or away from the Sun. But the Earth's axis has a second motion, rotating around a circle every 26,000 years. The impact of this 'precession' is that that the solstices and equinoxes shift slowly against the year as marked by the Earth's orbit around the Sun.

The precession of the Earth's axis affects the positions of the south and north celestial poles which move in circles, completing one circuit in approximately 26,000 years.

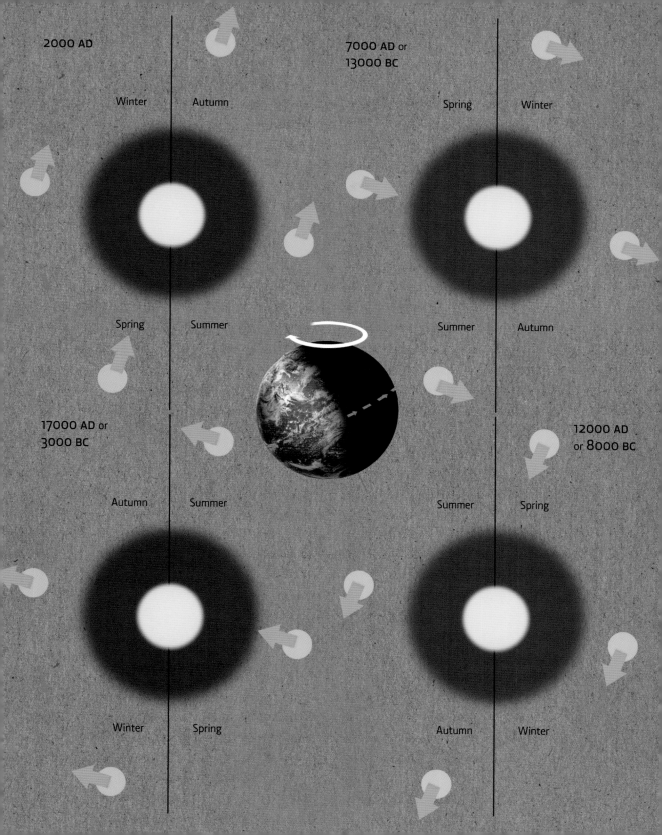

19 August 1646
Born in Denby, Derbyshire

1662
Begins programme of self-study on astronomy

1674
Awarded MA by Jesus College, Cambridge

1675
Appointed Astronomer Royal

1675
Ordained

1676
Observations begin at Greenwich Royal Observatory

1677
Elected Fellow of the Royal Society

1694
Begins correspondence with Newton over data on the Moon

1705
Begins work on astronomical catalogue

1711
Called by Newton in front of the council of the Royal Society to explain his behaviour

1712
Newton publishes a bootleg version of Flamsteed's catalogue, edited by Halley

1712 onwards
Burns up to 300 of the 400 copies of the pirated catalogue

31 December 1719
Dies in Greenwich

1725
Posthumous publication of Flamsteed's own star catalogue

JOHN FLAMSTEED

The last of Newton's significant scientific foes was John Flamsteed, whose career was damaged by their dispute over astronomical data.

The young Flamsteed may have been expected to go up to Oxford or Cambridge after attending a good school in Derby, but health problems led to a cancellation of university plans. Flamsteed's widowed father tried to prevent his son from following his interest in astronomy, but to no avail. Still in his teens, Flamsteed undertook a self-organized programme of reading and practical experience. He began making systematic observations in 1671, and at around the same time started writing to Henry Oldenburg and John Collins at the Royal Society.

New and influential friends Flamsteed made through the Society – notably mathematician and surveyor Jonas Moore, who became Flamsteed's patron – influenced King Charles II to get Flamsteed granted an MA from Jesus College, Cambridge, which he had briefly attended in 1674, and gained Flamsteed the position of the king's astronomical observator, known as the Astronomer Royal. The position brought with it a salary of £100 and a new observatory at Greenwich built to his specifications.

Flamsteed was also ordained around this time, enabling him to receive income from the living of Burstow in Surrey, though he would not take up the post until 1684. As an astronomer he worked on eclipses and comets, and was most famous for his star catalogue, a project that brought him under the influence of Newton. Flamsteed had come into some contact with Newton through the Royal Society, and was probably flattered to be asked to provide data for *Principia*, though less so when he discovered he received little credit for his contribution.

In the mid-1690s, Newton and Flamsteed began a correspondence during which their relationship went into decline. Flamsteed was already in dispute with Newton's great supporter Halley, over their competing tide tables. Now he took on a more dangerous foe. Newton demanded more and more data from Flamsteed, repeatedly criticizing the quality of the information so far supplied. After a brief respite when Newton moved to the Mint, more problems arose when Newton asked Prince George to commission an astronomical catalogue from Flamsteed, only to have Flamsteed's budget severely trimmed, as Newton did not require much of the information the Astronomer Royal hoped to include. The acrimonious and often public dispute dragged on for many years, with Flamsteed's final catalogue not published until after his death.

Brian Clegg

COMETS

the 30-second theory

RELATED TOPICS
See also
ORBITS
page 118

PLANETARY MOTION
page 136

3-SECOND THRASH
Newton showed that comets move on elliptical orbits just like planets – but rather than near-circular ellipses, these are highly elongated ones.

In the autumn of 1680 a comet appeared in the early morning sky. To earthbound observers, the comet seemed to travel in a straight line towards the Sun for a few days before disappearing from view. About a month later another much brighter comet appeared in the evening sky, this time heading away from the Sun. John Flamsteed, the Astronomer Royal, speculated that the two comets were actually one, and that its direction had been reversed by a kind of magnetic repulsion from the Sun. Newton considered Flamsteed's idea ludicrous; initially he rejected the idea of a single comet because he could see no other reason why it should change direction so dramatically. While he was working on the *Principia* a few years later, however, he realized that it was indeed a single comet – affected not by the Sun's magnetism but by its gravity. He argued that the comet was moving on a Keplerian ellipse just like a planet – but an ellipse that was so elongated that it could be approximated by an open curve called a parabola. In 1705, Edmund Halley used Newton's theory to predict that another comet – one seen in 1682 – would return again in 1758. The reappearance of Halley's Comet, right on schedule, was the first great demonstration of the predictive power of Newton's laws.

3-SECOND BIOGRAPHIES
JOHN FLAMSTEED
1646–1719
The first Astronomer Royal, who speculated about the nature of comets

EDMUND HALLEY
1656–1742
Flamsteed's successor, who predicted that the comet of 1682 would return in 1758

30-SECOND TEXT
Andrew May

3-MINUTE THOUGHT
The other distinctive feature of comets, besides the shape of their orbits, is their visual appearance. Unlike most astronomical objects, which tend to be round in shape, comets often have long tails that become increasingly pronounced in the vicinity of the Sun. Newton correctly theorized that the tail is made up of vapour given off by the solid nucleus as it is heated by the Sun.

Newton explained why a comet has a tail and the kind of elongated elliptical orbit comets take around the Sun; Halley then predicted the 1758 reappearance of the comet that takes his name.

APPENDICES

RESOURCES

BOOKS

*A Brief History of Infinity:
The Quest to Think the Unthinkable*
Brian Clegg
(Robinson Publishing, 2003)

A Brief History of Time
Stephen Hawking
(Bantam, 2011)

*Dark Matter: The Private Life of Sir
Isaac Newton*
Philip Kerr
(Three Rivers Press, 2003)

Isaac Newton
James Gleick
(Harper Perennial, 2004)

Isaac Newton: The Last Sorcerer
Michael White (Author)
(Fourth Estate, 1998)

Isaac Newton: Pocket Giants
Andrew May
(The History Press, 2015)

*The Mathematical Papers of Isaac
Newton*
Isaac Newton
(Cambridge University Press, 2008)

Newton and the Origin of Civilisation
Jed Buchwald and Mordechai Feingold
(Princeton University Press, 2012)

*Newton to Einstein: The Trail of Light:
An Excursion to the Wave-Particle
Duality and the Special Theory of
Relativity*
Ralph Baierlein
(Cambridge University Press, 2001)

The Optical Papers of Isaac Newton
Isaac Newton
(Cambridge University Press, 1984)

*Paradox: The Nine Greatest
Enigmas in Physics*
Jim Al-Khalili
(Black Swan, 2013)

Particle Physics: An Introduction
Frank Close
(Oxford University Press, 2004)

The Principia: Mathematical Principles of Natural Philosophy
Isaac Newton
(University of California Press, 1999)

The Scientific Worldview: Beyond Newton and Einstein
Glenn Borchardt
(iUniverse, 2004)

Why Does E=MC2?
Brian Cox and Jeff Forshaw
(De Capo, 2010)

WEBSITES

Eric Weisstein's World of Physics
scienceworld.wolfram.com/physics/

Frequently Asked Questions in Physics
math.ucr.edu/home/baez/physics/

University of Cambridge's digital library of Newton's papers
http://cudl.lib.cam.ac.uk/collections/newton

JOURNALS/ARTICLES

Man of Science, Man of God: Isaac Newton
Christine Dao
www.icr.org/article/newton

How Newton Changed the World
Heather Whipps
www.livescience.com/4965-isaac-newton-changed-world.html

RESOURCES

WORKS BY ISAAC NEWTON

De analysi per aequationes numero terminorum infinitas
(1669, published 1711)

Method of Fluxions
(1671)

Of Natures Obvious Laws & Processes in Vegetation
(unpublished, c. 1671–75)

De motu corporum in gyrum
(1684)

Philosophiæ Naturalis Principia Mathematica
(1687)

Opticks
(1704)

Reports as Master of the Mint
(1701–25)

Arithmetica Universalis
(1707)

Published posthumously

The System of the World
(1728)

Optical Lectures
(1728)

The Chronology of Ancient Kingdoms Amended
(1728)

De mundi systemate
(1728)

Observations on Daniel and The Apocalypse of St. John
(1733)

A Historical Account of Two Notable Corruptions of Scripture
(1754)

NOTES ON CONTRIBUTORS

Brian Clegg read natural sciences, specialising in experimental physics, at Cambridge and has a masters in Operational Research from Lancaster University. He spent a number of years at British Airways in high technology research and mathematical problem solving before forming a creativity consultancy, advising clients from the BBC to the Met Office. Since 2000 he has been a full time science writer with tiles including *Inflight Science*, *How to Build a Time Machine* and *The Quantum Age*. His *Dice World* and *A Brief History of Infinity* were both longlisted for the Royal Society Prize for Science Books. He gives regular talks at venues from the British Library and the Royal Institution to science festivals around the country. He is editor of book review site www.popularscience.co.uk and a Fellow of the Royal Society of Arts.

Simon Flynn studied chemistry at the University of Bristol and a Masters in philosophy at the University of York. He previously worked in publishing for fifteen years and is now a science teacher. Simon is the author of *The Science Magpie*.

Sophie Hebden is a freelance science writer based in Mansfield, UK. She combines writing about physics with looking after two small children. She has written for *New Scientist* and the Foundational Questions Institute, and is former news editor for SciDev.Net. She holds a PhD in space plasma physics, and a masters in science communication.

Andrew May is a technical consultant and freelance writer on subjects ranging from astronomy and quantum physics to defence analysis and military technology. After reading Natural Sciences at the University of Cambridge in the 1970s, he went on to gain a PhD in Astrophysics from the University of Manchester. Since then he has accumulated more than 30 years' worth of diverse experience in academia, the scientific civil service and private industry. His book *Isaac Newton: Pocket Giants* was published by the History Press in 2015.

INDEX

ACKNOWLEDGEMENTS

PICTURE CREDITS
The publisher would like to thank the following individuals and organizations for their kind permission to reproduce the images in this book. Every effort has been made to acknowledge the pictures; however, we apologize if there are any unintentional omissions.

All images from Shutterstock, Inc./www.shutterstock.com and Clipart Images/www.clipart.com unless stated.

Alamy/Cameni Images: 21T.
Alamy/Lebrecht Music and Arts Photo Library: 80, 85.
Alamy/North Wind Picture Archives: 31, 102.
Alamy/World History Archive: 21C.
NASA: 100.
Science Photo Library: 41.
Wellcome Library, London: 148.